For your country's sake today—

For your own sake tomorr[...]

GO TO THE NEAREST RECRUITING STATION
OF THE ARMED SERVICE OF YOUR CHOICE

LIPS
MIGHT
Sink Ships

[...]OMEONE

TALKE[...]

I WANT YO[...]

for the U.S. ARMY
ENLIST NO[...]

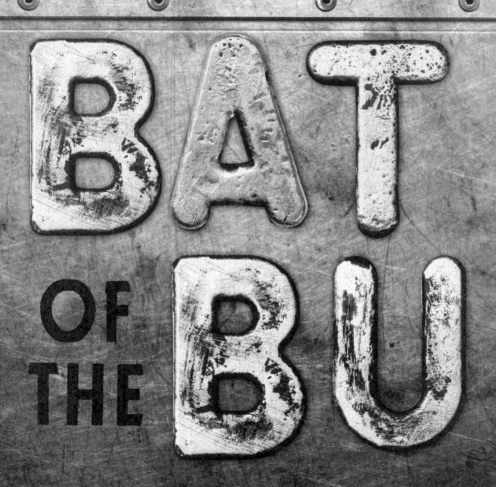

ADAPTED FROM *THE GUNS AT LAST LIGHT*

RICK ATKINSON

with KATE WATERS

SQUARE
FISH

HENRY HOLT AND COMPANY
NEW YORK

SQUARE
FISH

An Imprint of Macmillan
175 Fifth Avenue
New York, NY 10010
mackids.com

Square Fish and the Square Fish logo are trademarks of Macmillan and
are used by Henry Holt and Company, LLC under license from Macmillan.

Our books may be purchased in bulk for promotional, educational,
or business use. Please contact your local bookseller or the Macmillan Corporate
and Premium Sales Department at (800) 221-7945 ext. 5442 or by e-mail at
MacmillanSpecialMarkets@macmillan.com.

For a complete list of image credits, please see p. 247.

Library of Congress Cataloging-in-Publication Data
Atkinson, Rick.
Battle of the Bulge : adapted from The guns at last light / Rick Atkinson,
with Kate Waters.
pages   cm
Includes bibliographical references and index.
ISBN 978-1-250-07991-6 (paperback) — ISBN 978-1-62779-114-4 (ebook)
1. Ardennes, Battle of the, 1944–1945—Juvenile literature.
I. Waters, Kate.   II. Atkinson, Rick. Guns at last light.   III. Title.
D756.5.A7A78 2015   940.54'219348—dc23   2015000567

Originally published in the United States by Henry Holt and Company, LLC
First Square Fish Edition: 2016
Book designed by April Ward
Square Fish logo designed by Filomena Tuosto
Based on the book The Guns at Last Light by Rick Atkinson,
published by Henry Holt and Company, LLC.
Maps by Gene Thorp

1 3 5 7 9 10 8 6 4 2

AR: 9.0 / LEXILE: NC1270L

CONTENTS

MAP LEGEND

River/stream
HIGHWAY
MAJOR ROAD
MINOR ROAD /TRAIL
RAILROAD
WOODED
SWAMP
TERRAIN
△ HILL/MOUNTAIN
• City/town/village with urban area
✪ **Capital city**
○ Airfield
■ Landmark
Clash

UNITED STATES
UNITED KINGDOM
CANADA
GERMANY
FRANCE

	AXIS		ALLIED
Front line			
Airborne drop			
Advance			
Retreat			

TYPE OF UNIT

	Infantry	
	Armor	
	Mechanized	
	Armored cavalry	
	Airborne	
	Engineers	

GROUPS IN AN ARMY

I	Company
II	Battalion
III	Regiment
X	Brigade
XX	Division
XXX	Corps
XXXX	Army
XXXXX	Army Group

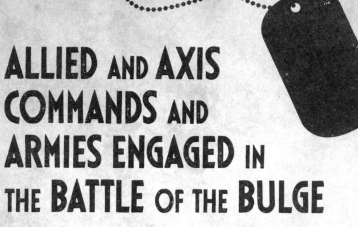

ALLIED AND AXIS COMMANDS AND ARMIES ENGAGED IN THE BATTLE OF THE BULGE

Army groups in italics fought the Battle of the Bulge.

ALLIES

- **DWIGHT D. EISENHOWER**, Supreme Commander of the Allied forces in Europe

BRITISH EMPIRE AND COMMONWEALTH

- **KING GEORGE VI**, King of the United Kingdom and Dominions of the British Commonwealth

CANADA

- **WILLIAM LYON MACKENZIE KING**, Prime Minister
- *GENERAL HENRY "HARRY" CRERAR—Canadian 1st Army*

UNITED KINGDOM OF GREAT BRITAIN AND NORTHERN IRELAND

- **WINSTON CHURCHILL**, Prime Minister
  - *FIELD MARSHAL BERNARD MONTGOMERY—British 21st Army Group*
  - *LIEUTENANT GENERAL MILES DEMPSEY—British 2nd Army, including XXX Corps*

UNITED STATES OF AMERICA

- FRANKLIN D. ROOSEVELT, President
  - GEORGE MARSHALL, General and Chief of Staff of the U.S. Army
  - *GENERAL OMAR BRADLEY—U.S. 12th Army Group*
    - *LIEUTENANT GENERAL COURTNEY HODGES—U.S. First Army*
    - *LIEUTENANT GENERAL GEORGE PATTON—U.S. Third Army*
    - *LIEUTENANT GENERAL WILLIAM SIMPSON—U.S. Ninth Army*

FREE FRENCH FORCES

- CHARLES DE GAULLE, leader of the Free French Forces, head of the French government in exile, and head of the French Army of Liberation
  - *MAJOR GENERAL JACQUES-PHILIPPE LECLERC, in command of Free French Forces in France*

AXIS

THE THIRD REICH (Nazi Germany)

- ADOLF HITLER, Führer
  - HEINRICH HIMMLER, Supreme Commander of the Home Army
  - *FIELD MARSHAL WALTER MODEL—German Army Group B*
    - *GENERAL HASSO VON MANTEUFFEL—German 5th Panzer Army*
    - *SS GENERAL JOSEF DIETRICH—German 6th Panzer Army*
    - *GENERAL ERICH BRANDENBERGER—German 7th Army*
  - *FIELD MARSHAL GERD VON RUNDSTEDT—German Army OB West*

WORLD WAR II TIMELINE

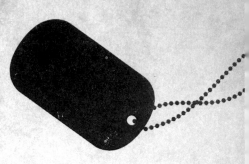

1939

MAY 22
Adolf Hitler of Germany signs a treaty with Italy's Benito Mussolini

AUGUST 23
Joseph Stalin of Russia and Adolf Hitler sign a pact vowing not to invade each other's countries

SEPTEMBER 1
Germany invades Poland

SEPTEMBER 3
Britain and France declare war on Germany

SEPTEMBER 10
The Parliament of Canada declares war on Germany

DECEMBER 18
First Canadian troops arrive in Europe

1940

APRIL 9
Germany invades Denmark and Norway

MAY 10
Germany invades Holland, Belgium, and Luxembourg

MAY 15
Holland surrenders

JUNE 10
Italy declares war on Britain and France

JUNE 14
Germany invades Paris, and France surrenders to the Nazis

JUNE 28
Charles de Gaulle is recognized as the leader of the Free French

Forces, French troops who had escaped to Britain after the Nazis occupied France

JULY 10
The Battle of Britain between the RAF and the Luftwaffe begins in the skies over England

SEPTEMBER 7
The German Blitz against Great Britain begins

SEPTEMBER 13
Italian forces invade Egypt

SEPTEMBER 17
Hitler postpones invasion of Britain after losing air battle

OCTOBER 7
German troops enter Romania

OCTOBER 28
Italy invades Greece

1941

APRIL 27
German troops occupy Athens

JUNE 1
The Nazi SS begin mass murder of Jews in eastern Poland

JUNE 22
Germans launch massive invasion of the Soviet Union

DECEMBER 7
The Japanese attack the U.S. naval base at Pearl Harbor, Hawaii

DECEMBER 8
The U.S. Congress declares war on Japan

DECEMBER 11
Germany and Italy declare war on the U.S. The U.S. Congress declares war on Germany and Italy

1942

JANUARY 26
U.S. troops arrive in Europe

FEBRUARY 15
The British surrender to Japanese forces in Singapore

APRIL 1
Internment of U.S. Japanese-American citizens begins

JUNE 4–7
The U.S. wins the decisive Battle of Midway, sinking four Japanese aircraft carriers

JULY 6
Anne Frank and her family go into hiding in Amsterdam

AUGUST
Germany attacks the Russian city of Stalingrad

NOVEMBER 8
The U.S. invasion of North Africa begins

1943

JANUARY 10
Soviets begin offensive against Germans in Stalingrad

JANUARY 23
U.S. troops take Tripoli (now Libya)

FEBRUARY 1
Germans surrender to Soviet forces in Stalingrad

MAY
Allied troops defeat the Germans in North Africa

JULY 5
Germans launch the largest tank battle in history at Kursk, Russia

JULY 9
Allied invasion of Sicily, an island off Italy, begins

JULY 25
Benito Mussolini is arrested, ending the Fascist regime in Italy

SEPTEMBER 8
Italy surrenders to the Allies; Hitler rushes troops to Italy

OCTOBER 13
Italy declares war on Germany

NOVEMBER 1
U.S. Marines land on the Japanese-occupied Solomon Islands in the Pacific Ocean

NOVEMBER 28
Roosevelt, Churchill, and Stalin meet in Yalta in Crimea to plan the final assault on and occupation of Germany

DECEMBER 1
Erwin Rommel becomes commander in chief of the German forces responsible for the defense of the Normandy coast

1944

JANUARY 17
Allies launch first attack against Germans in Italy

JANUARY 27
Soviet forces break the German 900-day siege of Leningrad, Russia, during which more than one million civilians died of starvation

FEBRUARY 20–25
German aircraft factories are bombed by U.S. and British air forces

MARCH 15
Germans launch offensive against India

APRIL 28
German E-boats attack Allied forces training for D-Day at Slapton Sands, England, killing nearly 700

JUNE 4
Allies liberate Rome, Italy, the first Axis capital to be freed after Canadians break the Hitler line south of the city

JUNE 6
D-Day

JULY 18
U.S. troops capture St.-Lô, France

JULY 21
U.S. Marines land on Japanese-occupied Guam in the Mariana Islands

JULY 29
Allies take Cherbourg, France

AUGUST 4
Anne Frank and her family are arrested

AUGUST 15
Allies launch the invasion of southern France

AUGUST 25
German troops in Paris surrender to the Allies

SEPTEMBER 3
The British liberate Brussels, the capital of Belgium

SEPTEMBER 17–22
Canadian Third Infantry Division liberates French ports of Boulogne and Calais

OCTOBER 20
U.S. invasion of the Philippines begins

OCTOBER 25
First Japanese kamikaze attack on a U.S. ship occurs

DECEMBER 16
The Battle of the Bulge begins

1945

JANUARY 17
Soviet troops capture Warsaw, Poland

JANUARY 25
The Battle of the Bulge ends

JANUARY 26
Soviet troops liberate the Auschwitz death camp in Poland

FEBRUARY 19
U.S. Marines begin the assault on the Japanese island of Iwo Jima

FEBRUARY 23
U.S. Marines raise the American flag on Mt. Suribachi, Iwo Jima

MARCH 7
U.S. troops cross into Germany on the Rhine River bridge at Remagen

MARCH 26
The battle for Iwo Jima ends

APRIL 1
U.S. troops land on the Japanese island of Okinawa

APRIL 11
U.S. troops liberate the Buchenwald concentration camp

APRIL 12
President Roosevelt dies suddenly; Harry Truman is sworn in as U.S. president

APRIL 15
British troops liberate the Bergen-Belsen camp, where Anne Frank and her sister died of typhus one month earlier

APRIL 30
Hitler commits suicide as Soviet troops approach Berlin

MAY 7
General Eisenhower accepts Germany's unconditional surrender

MAY 8
Germany surrenders to Russia

JUNE 5
Allies divide Germany into four zones

AUGUST 6
U.S. drops atomic bomb on the Japanese city of Hiroshima, killing as many as 140,000 people instantly

AUGUST 8
Soviet Union declares war on Japan

AUGUST 9
U.S. drops an atomic bomb on the Japanese city of Nagasaki, killing more than 80,000 people instantly

AUGUST 14
Japan surrenders

SEPTEMBER 2
Japan signs surrender agreement

SEPTEMBER 25
The Nazi Party is declared illegal in Germany

OCTOBER 24
The United Nations is created

NOVEMBER 13
General de Gaulle is elected president of France

NOVEMBER 14
The Nuremberg trials of Nazi leaders for war crimes begin

A more complete time-line, with videos, can be found at the Web site of the National World War II Museum at national-ww2museum.org. Canadian forces' efforts are described at the Canadian War Museum Web site at warmuseum.ca.

KEY PLAYERS

CLIFT ANDRUS: U.S. Major General, commander of the 1st Infantry Division

CHARLES BOGGESS: U.S. Lieutenant, 4th Armored Division

OMAR BRADLEY: U.S. General, commander of the 12th Army Group

ALAN BROOKE: British Field Marshal, Chairman of the British Chiefs of Staff Committee

CHARLES CAVENDER: U.S. Colonel, commander of the 423rd Infantry Regiment

WINSTON CHURCHILL: Prime Minister of the United Kingdom of Great Britain and Northern Ireland

BRUCE C. CLARKE: U.S. Brigadier General, 7th Armored Division

NORMAN "DUTCH" COTA: U.S. Major General, commander of the 28th Infantry Division

HENRY "HARRY" D. CRERAR: Canadian General, commander of the First Army

DERRILL M. DANIEL: U.S. Lieutenant Colonel, commander of the 2nd Battalion of the 26th Infantry Division

CHARLES DE GAULLE: French General, commander of the Free French Forces

FRANCIS "FREDDIE" DE GUINGAND: British Major General, Montgomery's chief of staff

MILES DEMPSEY: British Lieutenant General, Second Army commander

GEORGE L. DESCHENEAUX: U.S. Colonel, commander of the 422nd Infantry Regiment

JACOB DEVERS: U.S. Lieutenant General, commander of the 6th Army Group

MARK A. DEVINE, JR.: U.S. Colonel, group commander of the 14th Cavalry Group

JOSEF "SEPP" DIETRICH: German SS General, commander of the Sixth Panzer Army

DWIGHT D. "IKE" EISENHOWER: Supreme Commander of the Allied forces in Europe

MAMIE EISENHOWER: General Eisenhower's wife

HOMER D. FORD: U.S. Private First Class, 285th Field Artillery Observation Battalion

HURLEY E. FULLER: U.S. Colonel, regimental commander of the 110th Infantry

MARTHA GELLHORN: U.S. war correspondent

LEONARD GEROW: U.S. Major General, commander of V Corps

ROBERT W. HASBROUCK: U.S. Brigadier General, 7th Armored Division commander

FRIEDRICH VON DER HEYDTE: German Colonel, Dietrich's mission commander

ADOLF HITLER: Führer of Germany and leader of the Nazi Party

COURTNEY HODGES: U.S. Lieutenant General, First Army commander

WILLIAM M. HOGE: U.S. Brigadier General, 9th Armored Division

ALFRED JODL: German General, Hitler's operations chief

ALAN JONES: U.S. Major General of the 106th Infantry regiments

ALPHONSE JUIN: French military chief of staff

WILHELM KEITEL: German Field Marshal, chief of the German armed forces

OSCAR W. KOCH: U.S. Brigadier General, Patton's Third Army intelligence chief

HEINRICH VON LÜTTWITZ: German Lieutenant General, commander of XLVII Panzer Corps

HASSO VON MANTEUFFEL: German General, Fifth Panzer Army

GEORGE MARSHALL: Chief of Staff of the U.S. Army

ANTHONY CLEMENT MCAULIFFE: U.S. Brigadier General, 101st Airborne Division

TROY H. MIDDLETON: U.S. Major General, commander of VIII Corps

WALTER MODEL: German Field Marshal, Army Group B, one of two senior commanders in the west

BERNARD MONTGOMERY: British Field Marshal, commander of the 21st Army Group

ALAN MOOREHEAD: Australian war correspondent for London's *Daily Express*

JAMES E. PARKER: U.S. Captain, fighter pilot in the 4th Air Force

GEORGE PATTON: U.S. Lieutenant General, commander of the Third Army

JOACHIM PEIPER: German SS Lieutenant Colonel, commander of the 1st SS Panzer Regiment, part of the Sixth Panzer Army

FORREST POGUE: official U.S. Army historian

MATTHEW RIDGWAY: U.S. Major General, commander of the 82nd Airborne Division and leader of XVIII Airborne Corps

CHARLES P. ROLAND: U.S. Captain, 99th Infantry Division

FRANKLIN D. ROOSEVELT: President of the United States from March 1933 to April 1945

GERD VON RUNDSTEDT: German Field Marshal, one of two senior commanders in the west

WILLIAM SIMPSON: U.S. Lieutenant General in command of the Ninth Army

OTTO SKORZENY: German commando officer of the 150th Armored Brigade

BALDWIN B. SMITH: U.S. Lieutenant Colonel who served as Eisenhower's body double

WALTER BEDELL "BEETLE" SMITH: Eisenhower's chief of staff

KENNETH W. D. STRONG: British Major General, Eisenhower's intelligence chief

ARTHUR TEDDER: British Air Chief Marshal

HARRY TRUMAN: Thirty-third president of the United States

KURT VONNEGUT, JR.: U.S. Private First Class in the 423rd Infantry Regiment, future bestselling novelist

SIEGFRIED WESTPHAL: German General, Rundstedt's chief of staff

JOHN WHITELEY: British Major General, SHAEF deputy operations officer

A NOTE TO READERS

MY FATHER WAS A SOLDIER, which made me an "Army brat." He enlisted in the army when he was eighteen years old, in 1943, about halfway through World War II. He became a lieutenant and arrived in Europe just after the war there ended. A couple years later my father came home to America, went to college, got married, and went back into the army, this time to make it a career. Once again he was sent to war-torn Europe. I was born in Germany, but we lived for several years in Austria, which was still occupied by American troops.

I guess it's no wonder that I have always been fascinated by World War II. It was the worst catastrophe in human history—a time of great heroes, of bravery and sacrifice, but also a time of great villains, of cowardice and horrible crimes. Seventy years after it was fought, the war continues to influence our lives today. Whether or not your great-grandfather or great-grandmother served in the military or worked in a war factory, chances are it was the most exciting, terrifying, and memorable period of their lives.

World War II is also the greatest story of the twentieth century, and my hope is that you get to know this story because it tells us a lot about who we are as a nation and what events shaped the world you know today.

Washington, D.C.

March 1938: Adolf Hitler stands before a crowd at the Reichstag, or parliament, after Austria surrendered to the German army. The arms held up, hands palms down, was a form of salute.

Firefighters in London hose down burning buildings after a German bombing in 1941.

THE EUROPEAN THEATER

SEPTEMBER 1939–NOVEMBER 1944

THIS WAR, which in the end involved sixty-one countries, was sparked in September 1939 by Germany's invasion of Poland. Germany, under the leadership of Adolf Hitler, was determined to increase its size and resources. It had already absorbed Austria and Czechoslovakia, actions that provoked criticism but not war. Poland, however, was a country allied with most western European countries; therefore, Great Britain and France declared war on Germany.

THE GERMAN march west began soon after. In April 1940, Germany invaded Norway and Denmark, and the following month, Belgium and the Netherlands. As the armies of western Europe assembled and supplied for war, Germany began bombing

Britain, in raids known as the Blitz, German for "lightning." In less than a year, London was bombed seventy-one times, causing massive damage and resulting in the evacuation of hundreds of thousands of children to the countryside.

IN JUNE 1941, Germany turned the other way and invaded the Soviet Union.

It was the Japanese attack on the U.S. naval base at Pearl Harbor, Hawaii, in December 1941 that brought the United States into the conflict. Thus the sides were set: the Allied powers—including the United Kingdom, Canada, Australia, China, the Soviet Union, and the United States—against the main Axis powers of Germany, Italy, and Japan.

The U.S. destroyer Shaw *burns during the Japanese surprise bombing attack on the naval base at Pearl Harbor on the Hawaiian island of Oahu, December 7, 1941.*

Both Germany and the United States fought the war on two fronts: for Germany this meant European countries on the Western Front and the Soviet Union to the east. The United States fought on the European front against Germany and on the Pacific front against Japan.

ON JUNE 6, 1944, a massive assembly of ships and landing craft delivered 156,000 Allied troops to the beaches of Normandy, France. That intensified the slow, bloody effort to defeat the Germans on land and in the air. Town by town, Allied soldiers made their way across France to the German border. Along the way, they liberated Paris in August 1944, a significant defeat for the Germans and victory for the Allies. Finally, the Germans were driven back almost within their own borders. There, on December 16, 1944, Hitler initiated a last, desperate attack, hoping to retake much of Belgium and throttle the Allies' supply routes.

American troops approach the shores of Normandy, France, on D-Day, June 6, 1944.

American troops in a tank pass the Arc de Triomphe
during the liberation of Paris in August 1944.

EACH ARMY was hoping to outlast the other—outlast the
constant loss of troops while causing the enemy to lose heart
and surrender. After this final, savage six-week battle, Hitler
faced defeat. This is the story of the worst of war—of savagery,
deprivation, and despair—but also of astonishing bravery,
grit, and fortitude.

BOTH THE **ENEMY**
AND THE **WEATHER**
COULD **KILL YOU,**
AND THE TWO OF
THEM TOGETHER WAS
A **PRETTY DEADLY**
COMBINATION.

—BART HAGERMAN,
PRIVATE, 17TH AIRBORNE DIVISION

HITLER'

S PLAN

Hitler (seated, center) and his staff review plans for air strikes to support the Ardennes offensive.

Troops of the 17th Airborne Division move toward the front over snow-covered roads near Houffalize, Belgium, January 21, 1945.

STAKING
EVERYTHING
ON ONE CARD

DECEMBER 11, 1944

AN IRON-GRAY SKY rose above the gray-green Taunus Hills in Hesse, Germany, on Monday morning, December 11. A motorcade carrying German Führer Adolf Hitler and his staff of fifty officers and SS bodyguards rolled toward one of the remote headquarters the regime had built for itself in better days. The convoy sped south from the train station in Giessen toward Frankfurt for fifteen miles before turning west, past the heel-clicking sentries outside Ziegenberg Castle. The cars traveled a final mile beneath a camouflage canopy suspended from trees above the narrow road. With a crunch of tires on gravel, the convoy pulled to a stop, and the Führer climbed from the rear seat of his limousine, his face puffy and pale.

To the unschooled eye, the seven buildings of the Adlerhorst—the Eagle's Eyrie—resembled a small farming village, or perhaps a simple hunting camp. Several houses had wooden porches with flower baskets. Interior furnishings included oak floor lamps and tasseled shades; deer-antler trophies hung on the knotty-pine paneling. But a closer look revealed the cottages to be bunkers with thick concrete walls and reinforced roofs; the architect Albert Speer had designed them in 1939 as a field headquarters for officers directing military campaigns to the west of Germany. Some buildings were disguised as haystacks or barns, and a maze of subterranean passages with heavy metal doors and peepholes linked one building to another. Artificial trees were added to

Adlerhorst was built in the forest behind this castle.

the native conifers to create thick cover and prevent snooping by enemy aircraft. Hidden antiaircraft batteries ringed the compound. A concrete bunker half a mile long and masked as a brick retaining wall led across a shallow glen to Ziegenberg Castle, with its single stone tower dating to the twelfth century. After centuries of neglect, the castle had been refurbished in the 1800s, and in recent years, it had served as a rehabilitation hospital for wounded officers.

Hitler shuffled into his private chalet, known as Haus 1. The pronounced limp in his left leg was of mysterious origins. Doctors had recently removed an abscess from his vocal cords, and the long overnight trip from Berlin to Giessen aboard the Führer train, *Brandenburg,* had further exhausted him. "He seemed near collapse," one officer later wrote. "His shoulders drooped. His left arm shook as he walked."

In a few hours, he would unveil to his field commanders his planned masterstroke for snatching victory from his enemies. Destiny had brought him to this moment, to this dark wood, and he was ready, as his operations chief, General Alfred Jodl, put it, "to stake everything on one card." But first he needed rest.

DUSK ENFOLDED the Taunus Hills at five P.M., when two buses arrived at the compound. Heavy rain dripped from the pine boughs as a group of senior officers lined up to board. Many believed they had been summoned to the castle to toast Field Marshal Gerd von Rundstedt's sixty-ninth birthday on Tuesday, but a terse request that each man surrender his sidearm and briefcase at the guards' post suggested a less festive occasion. For half an hour, the buses lurched this way and that through the forest, the circuitous route intended to obscure the fact that they were traveling less than a mile across the glen to Haus 2, the Adlerhorst officers' club, connected by a covered walkway to the Führer's Haus 1.

A double row of armed SS guards formed a line from each bus to the club's main door; a steep flight of steps, now ringing beneath the heavy footfall of black boots, led to an underground situation room. As directed, each officer took his seat at a long rectangular table, with an SS man behind each chair in an attitude of such scowling intimidation that one general later admitted fearing "even to reach for a handkerchief." Rundstedt and Field Marshal Walter Model, the two senior German commanders in the west, sat impassively elbow to elbow.

SS soldiers stand guard in Munich, 1938.

Ten minutes later, Hitler hobbled in and sat with a grimace behind a small separate table at the head of the room, flanked by General Alfred Jodl and Field Marshal Wilhelm Keitel, chief of the German armed forces. The Führer's hands trembled as he pulled on his spectacles and picked up a sheaf of paper. Those who had not recently seen him were stunned by his appearance. One general wrote that he looked like "a broken man, with an unhealthy color, a caved-in appearance . . . sitting as if the burden of responsibility seemed to oppress him." Manipulating his dangling left arm with his right hand, "he often stared vacantly, his back was bent, and his shoulders sunken," another officer reported.

Then he spoke, and color flushed into his pale cheeks. His dull eyes once again seemed to kindle from within. For the first fifty minutes, he delivered a soaring lecture on history, fate, and how he had battled against "the policy of encirclement of Germany," devised by the British prime minister, Winston Churchill.

Never in history was there a coalition like that of our enemies, composed of such diverse elements with such different aims. Ultra-capitalist states on the one hand; ultra-Marxist states on the other. . . . Even now these states are at loggerheads. . . . These antagonisms grow stronger and stronger from hour to hour. If now we can deliver a few more heavy blows, then at any moment, this artificially bolstered common front may suddenly collapse with a gigantic clap of thunder.

Hitler believed that as the Allies approached one another, with Russian troops converging on Germany from the east and English, French, Canadian, and U.S. troops approaching from the west, the strain among the Allied nations would grow.

The palm of victory will in the end be given to the one who was not only ablest, but—and I want to emphasize this—was the most daring.

Toward that end he had a plan, originally code-named WACHT AM RHEIN (WATCH ON THE RHINE) but recently renamed HERBSTNEBEL (AUTUMN MIST). This he would now disclose on pain of death to any man who betrayed the grand secret.

It had come to him as in a fever dream, when he was sick in September. Brooding over what Jodl called "the evil fate hanging over us," the Führer had been hunched over his maps when his eye fixed on an unlikely seam through the Ardennes Forest—the mountain range spanned Luxembourg, Belgium, and France and connected to the Eifel range in Germany. Its rugged plateau was less than 2,500 feet high, but deep streambeds cut through the sixty miles between the German border and the Meuse River.

The Meuse River was the largest of the area's waterways. If the German army could cross it, they would have a chance of reaching Antwerp, the port city in Belgium that was the main entry point for all supplies for Allied troops in Europe. It could handle dozens of ships at a time, which, at the moment, were unloading more than a thousand tons of supplies a day for the Allies.

Hitler decided that for Germany to forestall the nation's imminent defeat, the enemy must be struck in one great, bold, and unexpected attack. A monstrous blow by two panzer armies could swiftly reach the Meuse bridges between Liège and Namur. If that plan succeeded, British Field Marshal Bernard Montgomery's 21st Army Group in the north would be separated from U.S. General Omar Bradley's 12th Army Group in the south. This would remove the enemy threat to the Ruhr region, Germany's industrial heartland. By destroying much of the Anglo-American strength in the west, Hitler believed he could require Churchill and U.S. President Franklin D. Roosevelt to sue for peace. As for the offensive's ultimate geographic objective, Hitler, in a conference with his senior generals, had abruptly blurted out a single word: "Antwerp."

THE SMALL SOLUTION

THE NAYSAYERS promptly said nay. To Rundstedt, who would command this great offensive, the Führer's order came as a "great surprise." Given the strained supplies of fuel, ammunition, and manpower, and with little support from the Luftwaffe, the German air force, Rundstedt concluded that the German force was "much, much, *much* too weak" to sustain a winter attack across 125 miles to Antwerp.

Rundstedt had told trusted aides, "The soldier can do nothing but buy time for the political leader to negotiate." His chief of staff, General Siegfried Westphal, wrote that "the entire planning of this offensive strikes me as failing to meet the demands of reality." Hitler brushed aside the objections, telling Rundstedt, "I think I am a better judge of this than you are, Field Marshal. I have come here to help you."

Even Model, who claimed to love those who craved the impossible, demurred, calling the Führer's scheme "damned moldy." The German Army Group B commander would provide most of the forces for AUTUMN MIST, and like Rundstedt, he considered Antwerp far too ambitious. Both men favored a slimmer plan—dubbed "the small solution," in contrast to Hitler's grandiose "large solution"—with a wheeling movement north around Aachen that would cut off the U.S. First and Ninth Armies and destroy ten to fifteen divisions. The two army commanders anointed by the Führer to lead the attack, Generals Hasso von Manteuffel and Josef "Sepp" Dietrich, had also endorsed the small solution in a six-hour conference with Hitler at the Reich Chancellery in Berlin on December 2. Not only was the small solution better suited to the force available, they argued, but German soldiers would fight desperately to reclaim the swatch of Germany now held by the Americans. That strip of hard-won territory fell between the German border and the German line of defense called the Siegfried Line.

The Commander in Chief of the German army in the west, Field Marshal Gerd von Rundstedt (right), and his top-level commanders, including Sepp Dietrich (third from right).

THE SIEGFRIED LINE CAMPAIGN
ALLIED MOVEMENT EAST
SEPT. 11–DEC. 15, 1944

North Sea

Ems R.

Miles
0   30   60

Kilometers
0   30   60

Amsterdam

NETHERLANDS

Rotterdam

Arnhem

Münster

Nijmegen

Front Line,
Dec. 15

West Wall

Wesel

Rhine R.

THE RUHR

Ruhr R.

XXXX
1
CRERAR

XXXX
2
DEMPSEY

Meuse R.

Venlo

XXXX
SCHLEMM

München-
Gladbach

Düsseldorf

GERMANY

Antwerp

Roer R.

Roermond

Front Line,
Sept. 11

MONTGOMERY
21st Army Group

XXXX
15
ZANGEN

Cologne

MODEL
Army Group B

Giessen

Brussels

Zonhoven

Maastricht

XXXX
9
SIMPSON

Jülich

Düren

Bonn

ADLERHORST

BELGIUM

Liège

Verviers

Aachen

HÜRTGEN
FOREST

Monschau

Remagen

RUNDSTEDT
OB West

Chaudfontaine

Spa

XXXX
6
DIETRICH

Frankfurt

Charleroi

Namur

Meuse R.

Huy

Aywaille

Manhay

Malmédy

Stavelot

Bütgenbach

Honsfeld

E I F E L

Koblenz

Mainz

Foy-Notre
Dame

Dinant

Sadzot

Vielsalm

St.-Vith

Prüm

XXXX
5
MANTEUFFEL

Mosel R.

Rhine R.

Givet

A R D E N N E S

XXXX
1
HODGES

Bitburg

Wittlich

Bastogne

Sauer R.

XXXX
7
BRANDEN-
BERGER

Neufchâteau

Diekirch

Our R.

West Wall

Trier

Mannheim

LUXEMBOURG

Luxembourg City

XXXX
1
OBSTFELDER

BRADLEY
12th Army Group

Meuse R.

Saarlautern

Saarbrücken

West Wall

Karlsruhe

Verdun

Front Line,
Sept. 11

Metz

XXXX
3
PATTON

Bitche

Front Line,
Dec. 15

Rhine R.

F R A N C E

DEVERS
6th Army
Group

XXXX
7
PATCH

Strasbourg

Gene Thorp

Map legend is on page vii.

"NOT TO BE ALTERED"

THE FÜHRER was unmoved. Only a brutal defeat would achieve the political objective of forcing the Anglo-Americans to the bargaining table. Only a dramatic victory could convince the enemy that the campaign was endless and hopeless. He promised thirty-eight divisions for the attack, supported by two thousand planes—planes he didn't have, since autumn fighting had whittled away German air strength. The final attack blueprint approved by Hitler on December 9 after the earlier conference in Berlin was virtually unchanged from the vision he had revealed earlier in the fall. A copy sent to Rundstedt was annotated by the Führer: *Not to Be Altered.*

In the Adlerhorst club's cellar that December 11, Hitler brought his two-hour oration to a close, eyes still bright, voice still strong. "The army must gain a victory. . . . The German people can no longer endure the heavy bombing attacks," he told the assembled officers. "We have many exhausted troops. The enemy also has exhausted troops, and he has lost a lot of blood." German intelligence estimated that the Americans alone "have lost about 240,000 men within a period of hardly three weeks." (This figure bore no relation to reality.) "Technically," he said, "both sides are equal."

The central weather office in Berlin predicted poor flying conditions over the Ardennes for a week; that would negate Allied air superiority. "Troops must act with brutality and show no human inhibitions," Hitler said. "A wave of fright and terror must precede the troops."

War is of course a test of endurance for those involved. . . . Wars are finally decided when one side or the other realizes that the war as such can no longer be won. Our most important task is to force the enemy to realize this. He can never reckon upon us surrendering. Never! Never!

Finally spent, Hitler ended his monologue. Rundstedt rose slowly from his chair. On behalf of his generals, he pledged loyalty to the Führer and vowed that they would not disappoint him, even though the field marshal had previously voiced "grave doubts" about this desperate scheme.

THE **SUPREME COMMANDER**

DECEMBER 12, 1944

SHORTLY BEFORE six P.M. on Tuesday, December 12, at roughly the hour that Hitler was repeating the previous night's oration for a second group of generals at the Adlerhorst, General Dwight D. "Ike" Eisenhower, supreme commander of the Allied forces in Europe, rode in a limousine through the dim streets of London toward the prime minister's residence at 10 Downing Street for a meeting with Winston Churchill and *his* military brain trust. Eisenhower had flown across the English Channel from his headquarters in Versailles, France, outside Paris, the previous day.

General Dwight D. Eisenhower, Supreme Allied Commander, on February 1, 1945.

As his car sped to the meeting, Eisenhower could see that London showed the devastation of war; all around were blown-out windows and crushed buildings. German V2 bombs continued to fall on the city, though none fell during Eisenhower's Tuesday night visit. At six P.M., Churchill welcomed the supreme commander to his map room, where they were joined by Air Chief Marshal Arthur Tedder, Field Marshal Alan Brooke, and several other senior British officers.

Eisenhower now commanded sixty-nine divisions on the Western Front, a force he expected to expand to eighty-one

From September 1940 until May 1941, the German Blitz targeted sixteen British cities. London was hit seventy-one times.

divisions by February. These soldiers, about fifteen thousand to a division, were from more than a dozen Allied nations. Using the prime minister's huge wall maps, upon which various battlefronts were outlined with pushpins and colored yarn, the supreme commander once again reviewed his campaign scheme for the ultimate defeat of Germany: how British Field Marshal Bernard Montgomery's 21st Army Group, bolstered by the U.S. Ninth Army under the command of Lieutenant General William Simpson, would angle north of the Ruhr Valley, while U.S. General Omar Bradley's 12th Army Group swung farther south, shielded on the right flank by U.S. Lieutenant General Jacob Devers's 6th Army Group. The two-sided threat would make the most of Allied mobility and force the enemy to burn his dwindling fuel stocks by defending a wide, perilous front.

In the face of some skepticism, Eisenhower explained his rationale with patience and coherence. Closing to the Rhine River from Holland to the Alsace region of France would give Allied forces the "capability of concentration" for an eventual double thrust. The fighting along the border in October and November had been grim—Allied troops still occupied only five hundred square miles of Germany—but German divisions were bleeding to death, and with them, the country.

The debate continued over cocktails and dinner, and the evening ended in stilted silences and muzzy talk about postwar Allied unity, to which the supreme commander pledged to devote "the afternoon and evening of my life." Churchill chimed in to endorse Eisenhower's broad-front concept. A day later, the prime minister asserted that he had simply been acting the gracious host in refusing to gang up on the only American at the table.

Eisenhower flew back to Versailles on Wednesday morning, weary and dispirited. In a letter to his wife, Mamie, he admitted craving a three-month vacation on a remote beach. "And oh, Lordy, Lordy," he added, "let it be sunny."

Eisenhower knew that every additional day of war left Britain weaker and less capable of preserving its empire or shaping the postwar world. "I greatly fear the dwindling of the British Army is a factor in France as it will affect our right to express our opinion upon strategic and other matters," Churchill had cabled Montgomery. German intelligence believed that fourteen British divisions still awaited deployment to the Continent, but the prime minister and Field Marshal Alan Brooke knew otherwise. Indeed, Britain was so hard-pressed that even after cannibalizing two existing divisions to fill the diminished ranks in other units, commanders faced "an acute problem in the next six months to keep the army up to strength," as one staff officer in London warned. Deaths and injuries among infantry riflemen especially were running at a rate higher than the War Office could replace: a British rifle-company officer who landed in France on June 6, 1944, had nearly a 70 percent probability of being wounded by the end of the war less than a year later, and a 20 percent chance of being killed.

Nor was Britain's plight unique. "All of us are now faced with an unanticipated shortage of manpower," Roosevelt had

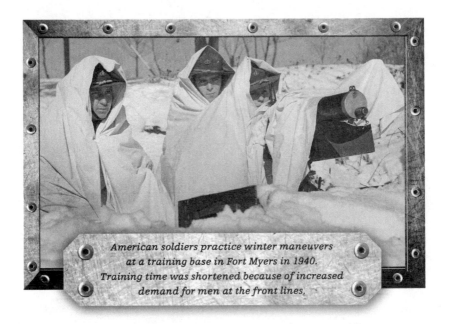

American soldiers practice winter maneuvers at a training base in Fort Myers in 1940. Training time was shortened because of increased demand for men at the front lines.

written Churchill in October. The American shortage was even more problematic because U.S. troops provided the majority of the Allies' troop strength. In December, the American armed forces comprised twelve million, compared with five million for the British. One million of those U.S. troops were now fighting the war on the Pacific front, while the Army Air Forces had requested 130,000 men to fly and maintain the new Boeing B-29 Superfortress bomber—beyond the 300,000 workers already building these heavy bombers at home.

The need for more soldiers—fit or unfit, willing or unwilling, whole or maimed—had grown ever more urgent as the fall months passed. Of more than eight million soldiers in the army as the year ended, barely two million were serving in ground units. That was simply not enough.

Now the army's ability to replenish its ranks was in jeopardy. On December 8, the Supreme Headquarters Allied Expeditionary Force, known as SHAEF, predicted a shortage of twenty-three thousand riflemen by year's end, enough to preclude any attack into Germany. On December 15, after returning from London, Eisenhower ordered units in the rear to send forward more combat troops, and an eight-week course to convert mortar crews and other infantrymen into riflemen was shortened to two weeks. At least a few officers wondered whether the time had come to allow black GIs to serve in white rifle companies, but even under these circumstances that radical notion found few champions in the high command.

Scouts wearing bedsheet camouflage patrol a snow-covered field in Luxembourg.

"I STILL HAVE NINE DAYS"

TO BE SURE, there were clues and omens. But the hints at what was to come were missed, ignored, or explained away. As a result, mistakes were made and many men died during the death struggle called the Battle of the Bulge. What might have been known was not known. What could have been done was not done. It was the worst U.S. intelligence failure since the Japanese surprise bombing of Pearl Harbor, and it was the deadliest of the war. Those bold character traits of warfare—valor, tenacity, composure—would be needed to make it right, as well as luck. The trial ahead would also require stupendous firepower and great loss of blood in what became the largest battle in American military history—and among the most decisive.

ALLIED INTELLIGENCE first recognized in September that the Germans had created the Sixth Panzer Army under a swashbuckling commander, General Sepp Dietrich. Also that month, an intercepted message from the ambassador of Germany's ally Japan described Hitler as intent on amassing a million new troops for combat in the west, "probably from November onwards." In late October, Ultra, the Allied intelligence project, revealed that the Luftwaffe was stockpiling fuel and ammunition at eleven airfields north of Aachen. Subsequent intelligence showed German aircraft strength in the west quadrupling, to perhaps 850 planes, reversing a policy of concentrating air squadrons defensively in Germany. Prisoner reports and a captured German order indicated that the celebrated enemy commando leader Otto Skorzeny was collecting soldiers who could "speak the American dialect," perhaps for an infiltration mission. The U.S. First Army had flown 361 reconnaissance sorties over western Germany since mid-November, spotting unusual processions of hooded lights on both banks of the Rhine, as well as hospital trains west of the river and canvas-covered flatcars apparently carrying tanks or trucks. In early December, Allied intelligence reported nearly two hundred German troop trains moving forward.

None of this suggested an enemy offensive, at least not to the minds of those scrutinizing the evidence. The German Sixth Panzer Army and the added Luftwaffe planes were seen as a counterattack force designed to shield the Ruhr but unable to mount a "true" counteroffensive—in SHAEF's judgment—because of fuel shortages and the German military's general weakness after extended warfare. An intercepted Luftwaffe order for aerial reconnaissance of bridges over the Meuse River, a site curiously far afield for those protecting only the Ruhr, was deemed a trick. A rumor of German intentions to recapture the port of Antwerp was dismissed in an intelligence review on December 3: "The bruited drive on Antwerp . . . is just not within his [Hitler's] potentiality." After all, hundreds of confirmed reports portrayed a battered, reeling foe.

Those nearest the front were the tactical units spread along the Siegfried Line. Hitler had built this 390-mile network of bunkers and tank traps along the western border of Germany. Allied forces watching for movement there also did not anticipate anything. Officers interviewing German prisoners

German infantry ride on a Tiger tank in early December 1944.

Hitler's defensive line of "dragons' teeth" was meant to stop tank advances.

in early December discounted reports of intensified training in infiltration techniques and assault tactics. Tanks maneuvering west of the Rhine were assumed to be green units undergoing seasoning, much as novice American units were seasoned in the Ardennes. A woman interrogated on December 14 described the forest near Bitburg as jammed with German equipment, and four German soldiers captured on December 15 reported more combat units arriving at the front, but these and various other clues provoked little alarm. None of the seven First Army divisions around the Ardennes foresaw an enemy offensive.

Several factors fed this disregard, including a failure to recognize that Hitler, rather than the prudent Field Marshal

Rundstedt, was directing German field armies in the west. It was thought that no sensible field marshal was likely to risk losing the Sixth Panzer Army—Germany's last mobile reserve in the area—in a winter offensive. In imagining their German counterparts, Forrest Pogue, the official U.S. Army historian, observed that American commanders believed that because "*we* would not attack under these conditions, therefore *they* would not attack under these conditions." To assume otherwise required the ability "to forecast the intentions of a maniac," General Bradley's intelligence chief later wrote.

Top Allied officers also had become overly enchanted with Ultra, the intelligence gathering and decoding initiative. By late 1944, the cryptologists at Ultra headquarters were daily providing about fifty intercepted German messages detailing troop movements and unit strengths. "They had become so dependent on Ultra that if it [a piece of information] wasn't there," a SHAEF officer said, "then there wasn't *anything* there." Intercepts had provided provocative clues—about those Luftwaffe planes on western airfields, for instance—and also raised troubling questions for those inclined to be troubled. Why were the Germans on the Italian front required to ship one thousand trucks west to Field Marshal Rundstedt? Why was Hitler's personal guard moving toward the Western Front? Why were German Sixth Panzer Army troop trains so far forward if Dietrich's mission was to protect the Ruhr River? But ruthless German security about AUTUMN MIST and strict radio silence by the units involved kept the secret from reaching Allied ears.

A suggestion in early December by Eisenhower's

German Tiger tanks ready for the Western Front.

intelligence chief, Major General Kenneth W. D. Strong, that the Sixth Panzer Army could possibly attack through the Ardennes sufficiently aroused Chief of Staff Walter Bedell "Beetle" Smith that he bundled Strong off to see General Bradley. In a forty-five-minute meeting in Luxembourg City, either Strong failed to convey a sense of alarm or Bradley refused to take counsel from his fears. The U.S. Army's VIII Corps was spread thin along the border, Bradley acknowledged, but ample reinforcements had been positioned behind the front, ready if needed. Bradley had apparently convinced himself that the enemy here lacked fangs: during a recent drive through the Ardennes, he had mused, "I don't think they will come through here. At least they can't do much here. Don't believe they will try." Back in Versailles, Strong recounted the conversation to Smith, who chose not to trouble Eisenhower with the matter.

Perhaps the only genuine prescience could be found farther south, where Lieutenant General George Patton and his Third Army intelligence chief, Brigadier General Oscar W. Koch, sensed what others did not: that a dangerous, desperate enemy remained capable of wreaking havoc. On December 7, Koch noted a "large panzer concentration west of the Rhine in the northern portion of Twelfth Army Group's zone of advance." Two days later, he pointed out the vulnerability of Major General Troy Middleton's VIII Corps in the Ardennes. It had been so quiet in VIII Corps' sector that it was used as a place to send soldiers for rest after heavy fighting on other fronts in Europe. On December 14, Koch cited the persistent mystery of the location of at least fourteen German divisions, most of them armored, which together could spearhead a counteroffensive. An attack near Aachen might be more likely than one through the Ardennes, he added, but Patton's intuition suggested otherwise. "The First Army is making a terrible mistake in leaving the VIII Corps static," he told his diary, "as it is highly probable that the Germans are building up east of them."

Yet in other Allied high councils, a confident swagger prevailed, a conviction that no German reserves would be committed west of the Siegfried Line. A "sudden attack in the West may with some certainty be said to have lapsed," British air intelligence concluded on December 6. "Attrition is steadily sapping the strength of German forces on the Western Front," the analysis declared, "and the crust of [German] defense is

Lieutenant General Patton and General Eisenhower confer over a map in 1944.

thinner, more brittle and more vulnerable." An abrupt enemy collapse seemed quite possible, and "given time and fair weather we can make progress against him anywhere."

On December 15, Montgomery wrote that Hitler's plight was so dire "that he cannot stage major offensive operations." That same day, the field marshal scribbled Eisenhower a note requesting leave to return to Britain for a few days. Montgomery included an invoice for a five-pound bet wagered in October 1943, when he had challenged Eisenhower's prediction that the war would end by Christmas 1944.

"I still have nine days," the supreme commander replied, "and while it seems almost certain that you will have an extra five pounds for Christmas, you will not get it until that day."

THE ARDENNES: "IT HAS BEEN VERY QUIET UP HERE..."

THE U.S. ARMY'S "Guide to the Cities of Belgium" assured soldiers that the Ardennes was a fine place "to practice your favorite winter sport." The region was said to have become a "quiet paradise for weary troops."

Of the 341,000 soldiers in the U.S. First Army, 68,822 were in VIII Corps, anchoring the army's right flank with three divisions in the line. They held an eighty-five-mile front—three times the length advised for a force of such strength under army tactical doctrine—that snaked down the Belgian border through Luxembourg to Patton's Third Army's sector. At two spots, the line crossed the border into Germany's Schnee Eifel, a snowy ridge that was a topographical extension of the Belgian Ardennes. Intelligence officers calculated that 24,000 enemy soldiers currently faced VIII Corps, so few that the First Army had recently ordered a deception program to feign an American buildup in the Ardennes; the intent was to lure

Troops of the U.S. 17th Airborne Division move toward the front near Houffalize, Belgium, in January, 1945.

more Germans, weakening Rundstedt's lines to the north and south. Some VIII Corps troops wore phony shoulder flashes, drove trucks with bogus unit markings, broadcast counterfeit radio traffic, and played recordings of congregating tanks— all to suggest an amassing of strength that was not taking place. In reality, some infantry regiments that typically should have held a 3,500-yard (two-mile) front in such broken country now were required to hold frontages of six miles or more.

For much of the fall, four veteran U.S. divisions had occupied the Ardennes, mastering the terrain and rehearsing both withdrawal and counterattack plans. But in recent weeks, they had been replaced by two bloodied divisions from the battle of Hürtgen Forest—those weary troops seeking a quiet paradise—and the newly arrived 106th Infantry Division, which was not only the greenest army unit in Europe but also the youngest. This was the first division into combat with substantial numbers of eighteen-year-old draftees. As with so many newer divisions, the 106th had trained diligently for months at home. After arriving at Le Havre, France, on December 6, the 106th had been trucked across France to reach the Ardennes front at seven P.M. on December 11, "numb, soaked, and frozen," as a military historian later wrote. Man for man, foxhole for foxhole, across a twenty-eight-mile sector, they replaced troops of the 2nd Infantry Division, who bolted west for showers and hot food in the rear.

American infantrymen line up for chow in Germany's Hürtgen Forest, January 2, 1945.

Few soldiers of the 106th had ever heard a shot fired in anger, and some failed to adjust their rifles to ensure accurate marksmanship, something that should have been done daily. Radio silence precluded the testing and calibration of new communication sets. Battalions reported shortages of winter clothing, maps, machine-gun tripods, and mortar, antitank, and bazooka ammunition. The dreaded disease trench foot soon spiked when green troops neglected to dry their socks properly. Despite orders to mount an "aggressive defense," few patrols ventured forward, and German war dogs terrorized those who did.

"The woods are of tall pines, dark and gloomy inside. After a snow it is all in black and white," an artilleryman wrote his wife from an outpost near the Losheim Gap. A departing 2nd Division colonel told his 106th replacement, "It has been very quiet up here and your men will learn the easy way."

THE PLAN WAS FIXED

HITLER'S PLAN, the one marked "not to be altered," was designed to create a wedge in Allied defenses and thereby allow German forces to break through Allied lines, cross the Meuse River, and march to Antwerp. Two tank armies would form the point of a spear, with the Sixth Panzer Army under the command of General Sepp Dietrich on the right, or north, and General Hasso von Manteuffel's Fifth Panzer Army on the left, or south.

Dietrich's goal was to funnel into Belgium through the five-mile-wide Losheim Gap, then hurry down five major roads to reach the Meuse River near the town of Liège and turn northwest for Antwerp.

Manteuffel was directed to sweep to the Meuse through southern Belgium and Luxembourg, shielding Dietrich's flank against attack from the Americans.

If successful, the campaign would separate Montgomery's

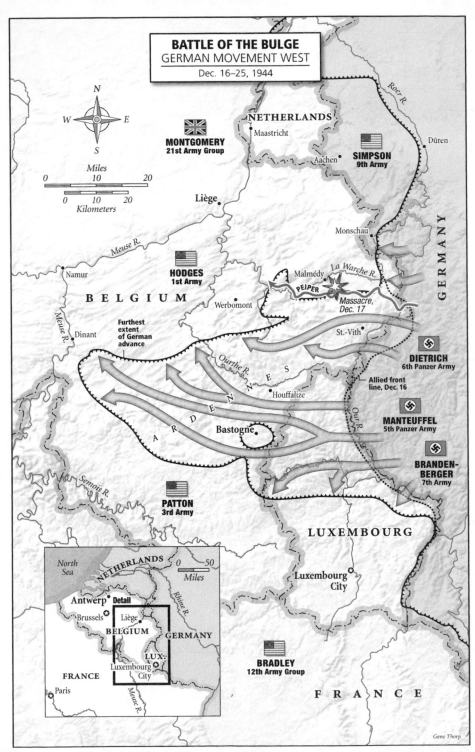

Map legend is on page vii.

21st Army Group in the north from the Americans in the south. These massive German armies would attack across a front that was one hundred miles wide. The armies in front numbered two hundred thousand men, with two thousand artillery pieces and almost one thousand tanks and assault guns. These would try to take on not only the Allied armies but also the Ardennes, one of the most rugged terrains north of the Alps.

Hitler had been consumed for weeks by the minutest details of the plans—from providing at least three blankets to each shock trooper, those who would lead the attack, to banishing Alsatian troops from frontline units as security risks. (They were mustered from a conquered area of France.) Hitler ordered

The German army depended on horsepower to do much of its pulling and carrying. Only one-fifth of the German army was mechanized. Here, camouflaged supply wagons head to the front.

Heinrich Himmler, supreme commander of the Home Army, to round up two thousand horses to increase mobility.

Beginning in early December, a thousand trains had hauled the AUTUMN MIST legions across the Rhine, where they disembarked at night between Trier and München-Gladbach, then marched in darkness toward the front. Security remained paramount. No open fires were allowed, to minimize detection. Any officer initiated into the plan took multiple secrecy oaths and then was forbidden to travel by airplane, lest he be shot down and captured. Agents for the Gestapo, Germany's secret police, sniffed for leaks.

Maps remained sealed until the last moment. To forestall deserters, only on the final night would shock troops move into their assault trenches. Low-flying planes buzzing overhead provided "noise curtains" to conceal ground engine sounds. The attack, originally scheduled for late November and then postponed until December 10, had been delayed again for nearly a week to stockpile more fuel and permit further positioning. *Null Tag*—Zero Day—now was fixed for Saturday, December 16, the date celebrated as the birthday of that most exquisite German, the composer Ludwig van Beethoven.

THE GERMANS' FINAL ASSEMBLY AREA

DECEMBER 15, 1944

STRAW AND RAGS muffled gun wheels and horses' hooves as twenty German divisions lumbered into their final assembly areas on Friday night, December 15. Breakdown crews with tow trucks stood ready along roads that now carried only one-way traffic, and military policemen were authorized to shoot out the tires of any vehicle violating march discipline. For the last kilometer leading to the line of departure, soldiers carried ammunition by hand or on their backs. Quartermasters issued ration packets of "special vitalizing and strengthening foods," including fifty grams of genuine coffee, grape-sugar tablets, chocolate, fruit bars, and milk powder. "Some believe in living but life is not everything!" a soldier from the German 12th SS Panzer Division wrote his sister. "It is enough to know that we attack and will throw the enemy from our homeland. It is a holy task."

Two hundred thousand German assault troops packed

into an assembly area three miles deep. The initial blow by seven panzer divisions and thirteen infantry, bolstered by almost two thousand artillery tubes and a thousand tanks and assault guns, would fall on a front sixty-one miles wide. Five more divisions and two brigades waited in the second wave, giving the Germans roughly a five-to-one advantage over the opposing U.S. forces in artillery and a three-to-one edge in armor. The best of Rundstedt's divisions had 80 percent of their full complement of equipment; others, but half. Panzer columns carried enough fuel to travel one hundred miles under normal cruising conditions, which existed nowhere in the steep, icy Ardennes. Few spare parts or antitank guns were to be had, but for a holy task, perhaps none were needed.

Hitler had indeed staked the future of his nation on one card. The final diary entry of the German army command in the west that Friday night declared, "Tomorrow brings the beginning of a new chapter in the campaign in the West."

This photograph, captured from the Germans, shows a German soldier carrying ammunition toward the front lines.

Soldiers of the U.S. 82nd Airborne Division gather around a fire in the Ardennes Forest.

"NOTHING TO REPORT"

IN THE RED-ROOFED Belgian army barracks that served as the VIII Corps command post in the town of Bastogne, champagne corks popped on Friday night to commemorate the anniversary of the corps' arrival in Britain a year earlier. The commander, Major General Troy Middleton, had reason to be proud of his men's combat record. He drank a final toast to battles past and future before retiring to his sleeping van.

A few miles to the east, the faint clop of horses and a growl of engines in low gear drifted to American soldiers on watch duty along the Our River, which marks the border between Luxembourg and Germany. Their report of disturbing noises in the night traveled up the chain of command from one headquarters to the next, with no more heed paid than had been paid to earlier intelligence. Middleton's command post in Bastogne issued a weather forecast for Saturday—"Cloudy, snow beginning around 1300. Visibility 2 miles"—and a three-word battle summary for the Ardennes: "Nothing to report."

ZERO

DAY

DECEMBER 16, 1944

German Panther V tanks on a road in the Ardennes.

SS infantry advance as the attack begins.

THIS HAUNTED PLATEAU

SHEETS OF FLAME leaped from the German gun pits at precisely 5:30 A.M. on December 16. Drumfire fell in crimson splashes across the front with a stink of turned earth and burned powder, and the green fireballs of 88mm shells bored through the darkness at half a mile per second, as if hugging the Ardennes hills. The shriek of German Nebelwerfer rockets—known as Screaming Meemies—echoed in the hollows where wide-eyed GIs crouched. Then enemy machine guns added their racket to the din, and rounds with the heft of railroad spikes splintered tree limbs and soldiers' bones alike. The thrum of panzer engines now could be heard from the east, along with a creak of armor wheels, and as the artillery crashed and heaved, a rifleman in the U.S. 99th Infantry Division reflected, "You'd think the end of the world is coming."

Through the trees the infantry emerged as bent shadows, some in snowsuits or white capes, others in green greatcoats with helmets or duckbill caps, shouting and singing above the whip-crack of rifle fire. One GI, hiding in a barn among cows, whispered, "The whole German army's here." Along the thin American line, men dug in deeper, scratching furrows with helmets and mess tins. Others scuttled to the rear, past the first dead men, who wore the usual blank expressions.

The battle was joined, this last great grapple of the Western Front, although hours would elapse before American commanders realized that the opening barrage was more than a deception, and days would pass before some generals acknowledged the truth of what Rundstedt had told his legions in an order captured early Saturday: *Es geht um das Ganze.* Everything is at stake.

The struggle would last for a month, embroiling more than a million men drawn from across half a continent to this haunted plateau. The first act of the drama, perhaps the most decisive, played out simultaneously across three bloody fields scattered over sixty miles—on the American left, on the American right, and in the calamitous center. "Your great hour has struck," Rundstedt had declared to his men. "You bear in yourselves a divine duty to give everything and to achieve the superhuman for our Fatherland and our Führer."

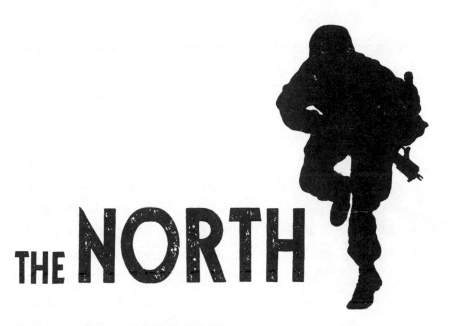

THE NORTH

THE ATROCITIES BEGIN

NO MAN embraced Field Marshal Rundstedt's sentiments with greater fervor than the slender young SS lieutenant colonel barking at the jammed traffic northwest of the Losheim Gap on Saturday morning. Joachim Peiper's great hour had indeed struck, yet he was already late. A highway bridge across a rail cut had been demolished in September by retreating German troops, but now engineers assigned to repair the span could not get past the mule wagons, horse-drawn artillery carriages, and Tiger tanks clogging the narrow road. The stalled column of tanks and personnel carriers snaked for miles back into Germany.

As commander of the First SS Panzer Regiment, proudly wearing the death's-head insignia above the visor of his peaked cap, Peiper had been given the specific duty of

German SS Lieutenant Colonel Joachim Peiper. The skull insignia on his hat is called a totenkopf.

streaking across Belgium with a task force of almost six thousand men and seventy-two tanks to seize the Meuse River crossings at Huy, Belgium. Although only twenty-nine, he was an obvious choice as the *Spitze*—the point—of the Sixth Panzer Army's attack and, indeed, all of AUTUMN MIST. He was a Berliner born into a military family, fluent in English and French. Much of his war had been spent in the east, burning villages and slaughtering civilians with such abandon that his unit was nicknamed the Blowtorch Battalion. Two of his brothers, also SS men, were now dead, but Peiper's devotion to Germany was undimmed. With Allied bombers terrorizing German cities, he did not question Hitler's orders to wield fear and terror as weapons.

In early December, after a test run in a Panther tank near Bonn, Germany, Peiper reported that a tank regiment could cover eighty kilometers in a single night, "if I had a free road to myself." But when assigned his route to the Meuse in December, he had complained that "these roads were not for tanks but for bicycles." Finally, at 7:30 P.M., the stalled column found a detour through Losheim.

More troubles awaited. Both German and American mines

cost Peiper five tanks before the task force reached Lanzerath at midnight; an hour later, he ordered two Panthers to take the point, guided through the dark woods by troops waving white handkerchiefs so as to be seen in the darkness.

Shortly before six A.M. on Sunday, the *Spitze* clattered into Honsfeld to find American vehicles parked in doorways and exhausted GIs sleeping inside. Here the atrocities began. Eight soldiers rousted outside in their underwear and bare feet, shouting "Comrade, I surrender," were lined up in the street and murdered with a machine gun. Five others emerged from a house with a white flag; four were shot, and the fifth, pleading for mercy, was crushed beneath a tank. Four more Americans, also carrying a large white banner, were shot. Peiper's men stripped boots from the dead and pressed on to Büllingen, two miles northwest.

German intelligence had correctly identified Büllingen as a likely Allied fuel dump, and SS crews, after raking a dozen parked spotter planes with gunfire on an airstrip outside town, seized fifty thousand gallons of gasoline by ten A.M. Two hundred men were rounded up. Before being marched to prison cages in the rear, GIs were forced to fill the panzers' gas tanks in the town square, which in happier days had served as a cattle market. Already many hours behind schedule and still sixty miles from Huy, with orders to ignore his exposed flanks and all diversions, Peiper now pivoted southwest—unwittingly giving the Americans a priceless tactical reprieve. Had he swung northwest a few miles to Bütgenbach and then Elsenborn, where the 12th SS Panzer Division was attacking from the east, he likely would have

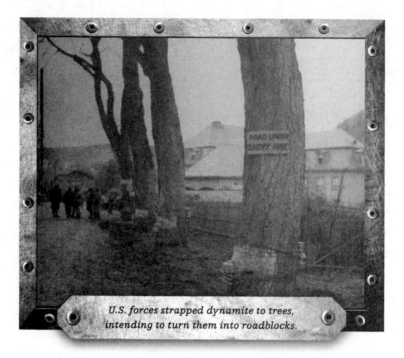

U.S. forces strapped dynamite to trees,
intending to turn them into roadblocks.

encircled as many as thirty thousand GIs who were strug-
gling to fall back to defensible ground.

This serendipity proved catastrophic for Battery B of the
U.S. 285th Field Artillery Observation Battalion, which early
that morning had hurriedly decamped from Germany with
orders to move to Luxembourg. At 11:45 A.M., 140 men in
thirty-three vehicles stopped for a Sunday lunch of hash,
peas, and pineapple outside the town of Malmédy, ten miles
west of Büllingen. An hour later, the march south resumed,
past army engineers taping TNT to ash trees to be blown
down as roadblocks if necessary. As the convoy sped through
Malmédy on Highway N-23, Belgian civilians gestured ahead,
yelling the slang term for German soldiers, *"Boches! Boches!"*

Boches there were, and in a particularly foul mood after

clumping down a barely passable muddy animal trail. Three miles below Malmédy, at the crossroads hamlet of Baugnez, Peiper's SS column collided with Battery B shortly before one P.M. For two minutes, German machine-gun and tank fire peppered the American convoy, until Peiper, furious at the destruction of fifteen fine U.S. trucks, managed to call a cease-fire. A few GIs had been killed, a few others escaped through the woods or hid in ditches, but more than one hundred surrendered, some with white rags tied to their rifle barrels. As Panthers shoved the burning trucks off the road, prisoners were herded with hands high into eight rows on a snowy field, where their captors stripped them of rings, cigarettes, watches, and gloves. Peiper watched for a few minutes from his personnel carrier, then pushed on down the N-23 highway toward Ligneuville.

No one would ever be certain which German soldier fired the first shot, but at 2:15 P.M., an abrupt fusillade from two panzer machine guns chewed into the ranks of prisoners still standing with their hands raised. "At the first outburst of fire, everyone fell to the ground, including myself," recalled Private First Class Homer D. Ford, a military policeman who had been captured while directing traffic at the crossroads. Ford lived to describe the horror:

> I was wounded in the left arm while the group was being sprayed on the ground. . . . I was laying in the snow . . . and I was afraid they would see me shivering but they didn't. . . . I could hear them pull the trigger back and then the click.

For twenty minutes, executioners prowled the field. An American medic permitted to attend a wounded soldier was then shot along with his patient. A dozen GIs who had fled into a scruffy café at the crossroads were flushed when the building was set ablaze and shot down as they scattered. For the next two hours, passing SS convoys fired into the mounded bodies until even the SS tired of the sport.

Unaware for the moment that his troops had just committed one of the most infamous battlefield crimes of the war, Peiper arrived at Ligneuville in midafternoon. He was disappointed to find that American officers had just fled, but he spent thirty minutes wolfing down the lunch they had left behind in the dining room of the Hôtel du Moulin. Here a German sergeant led eight U.S. prisoners out back to dig graves for three dead Germans; he then shot the Americans in the head, killing seven.

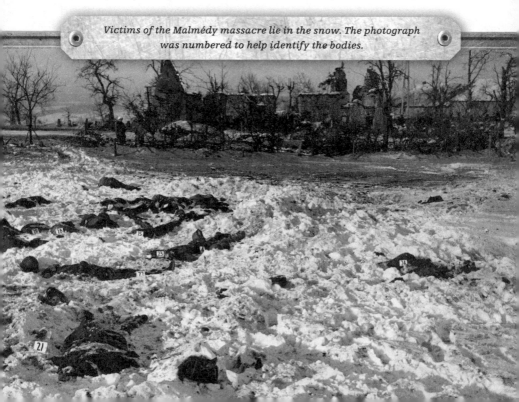

Victims of the Malmédy massacre lie in the snow. The photograph was numbered to help identify the bodies.

The eighth fled bleeding through the forest, only to be later captured again and sent to a prisoner-of-war camp.

THE *SPITZE* pushed westward that Sunday, December 17. Twilight had fallen when Peiper reached the wooded bluff above Stavelot on the Amblève River. A single squad of American combat engineers held the town, but when three panzers rushed the only bridge, a mine crippled the lead tank, giving Peiper pause. Perhaps the defenders were stronger than he realized. His march column, strung out for fifteen miles across Belgium, would have to close ranks for an assault into Stavelot, and after three nights of little sleep, his men desperately needed rest. He gave the order: they would halt until dawn. They were still forty-two miles from the Meuse.

Behind him, near Malmédy, more than eighty corpses lay in the snow. But at least a dozen GIs had pretended to be dead for more than two hours, and now they rose and ran through the woods. Soon word of the massacre passed from foxhole to foxhole and up the chain of command, reaching U.S. First Army headquarters in the Belgian town of Spa even before Peiper decided to stop for the night. Vows to give no quarter spread through the ranks; there were formal decrees in at least two regiments. "American troops are now refusing to take any more SS prisoners," the Ninth Army war diary would note, "and it may well spread to include all German soldiers." Everything was at stake.

Peiper had bored a small, vicious hole through the American left flank, but that opening would have to be widened considerably if the bulk of General Dietrich's Sixth

American soldiers uncover bodies of soldiers shot by the SS at Malmédy.

Panzer Army was to ram through. Much of the weight of Dietrich's attack fell on the U.S. 99th Infantry Division, another inexperienced unit that had been wedged into a twenty-mile swatch of the Ardennes front, between Monschau in the north and Lanzerath in the south. By Sunday morning, various battalions had been chopped to pieces in what Captain Charles P. Roland called "a red nightmare," and much of the division reeled west in confusion. Soldiers siphoned gasoline from wrecked jeeps to ignite flame pits across forest trails, but the enemy came on, bayoneting GIs in their holes and firing point-blank through cellar windows.

Artillerymen spiked their discarded guns with thermite grenades, and drivers opened radiator valves to drain the antifreeze before abandoning their trucks to flee on foot through the woods. Signalmen smashed switchboards, adjutants burned secrets, and skittish soldiers shot one another by mistake, including one clutch of GIs who accidentally killed their own major, then wounded a captain who was trying to calm them down.

Three miles from the German border, the twin Belgian villages of Krinkelt and Rocherath stood in the path of the German 12th SS Panzer Division. The Murder Division, it was called, because it had been responsible for liquidating so many Canadian prisoners during the Allied invasion of Normandy in June. Two panzer grenadier battalions probed the villages on Sunday, only to butt against veterans from the

Bazookas fired successfully in the cold, snowy environment.

U.S. 2nd Infantry Division who had been hustled into the line so quickly that some had Christmas packages from home dangling on their belts and rifle barrels; one witness thought they looked "more like postmen than soldiers."

A full-throated German assault at first light on Monday, December 18, failed to get through, and fighting swept from house to house, room to room, alley to muddy alley, with grenades, knives, tank destroyers, and artillery fire. Smoke spiraled up in thick braids as men from both sides were captured, freed, and recaptured. Antitank guns and bazooka teams, along with almost thirty thousand artillery rounds, knocked out so many German Panthers that a German officer called the villages "a perfect panzer graveyard." An enemy strategy to outflank the American line by attacking through Höfen, ten miles north, ended with the corpses of a battalion of German Volksgrenadiers littering the snow like gray stepping-stones. Burial details tallied 554 German bodies and only a dozen U.S. casualties.

German soldiers abandon their tank and surrender.

"MUCH HAPPENING OUT THERE"

DECEMBER 19, 1944

AT DUSK ON Tuesday, with the last remnants of the 99th Infantry Division bundled to the rear except for stouthearts fighting with the 2nd Infantry Division, the Americans slipped from Krinkelt and Rocherath in thick fog, abandoning those flaming towns for better ground a thousand yards west—a curved crest two thousand feet high, running from southwest to northeast and unmarked on Belgian military maps. American commanders named this high ground after a nearby village: Elsenborn Ridge. Here Major General Leonard Gerow, the V Corps commander, believed the German attack could impale itself.

V Corps gunners muscled 90mm antiaircraft guns to be used as artillery onto the ridge. Troops shoveled dirt into empty wooden ammunition boxes for field fortifications and burrowed down in the shale slope, roofing the hollows with pine logs and doors ripped from their hinges in a nearby Belgian barracks. Riflemen from the 2nd Infantry Division filled the ridgeline on the right and those from the 99th held the left, braced by the veteran 9th Infantry Division taking positions below Monschau in the north. An officer described a command post near Elsenborn as "a big crowd of officers, all with map cases, binoculars, gas masks, etc., milling about. Nobody knew anything useful, even where the enemy was."

Here, for three days and nights, German paratroopers and the 12th SS Panzer Division smashed against the defensive bulkhead again and again. One message from the U.S. 1st Infantry Division to their commanding officer Major General Clift Andrus's headquarters advised, "Attack repulsed. Send litters." Then: "Much happening out there. We are killing lots of Germans."

U.S. man power moves this cannon gun through the mud on the German–Belgian front line.

German tanks were called panzerkampfwagens, *meaning "armored combat vehicles."*

The heaviest blows fell on the 26th Infantry Division's 2nd Battalion, commanded by Lieutenant Colonel Derrill M. Daniel. On Wednesday, his men withstood a night attack by twenty truckloads of whooping German infantry supported by panzers churning through mud, and a rampage of machine-gun and 75mm fire by eight Panthers. Thursday brought worse yet, with a three-hour cannonade before dawn by German howitzers and Nebelwerfers; then two battalions of German paratroopers and SS panzer grenadiers spilled from a pine wood in the west, trailed by thirty panzers. The 2nd Battalion's right flank crumbled, and SS tanks wheeled up and down the line, crushing GIs in their foxholes.

"Get me all the damned artillery you can get," Daniel radioed. Ten thousand rounds in eight hours—among the fiercest concentrations in the European war—kept enemy infantry at bay, but panzers closed to within a hundred yards of the battalion command post in a farm compound. For much of the day, Daniel and his staff crouched in a cellar with the wounded, burning classified papers as tank and machine-gun rounds blistered the four-foot-thick stone walls. Sleeting counterfire from American Sherman tanks and the new 90mm tank destroyers finally evicted the last attackers from behind a barn by shooting right through it; only one panzer escaped. An eerie silence descended with the night.

Army patrols reported enemy dead "as common as grass," and grave diggers would count nearly eight hundred bodies,

Debris left at an Allied gun position on Elsenborn Ridge.

along with the wrecked hulks of forty-seven panzers and self-propelled guns. During the protracted fight at Elsenborn Ridge, five thousand were killed, wounded, or went missing in the U.S. 2nd and 99th Infantry Divisions alone.

But the American line held. Here the Sixth Panzer Army reached its high-water mark, as far as it would get on the north shoulder of what came to be called "the bulge," that fifty-mile-wide area of Belgium and Luxembourg that the Germans occupied for a month in the winter of 1944–45. General Dietrich needed an eight- to twelve-mile cushion on his right flank to keep his German assault columns out of range of American artillery as they lumbered toward the Meuse. Instead, his troops were forced to move away from the main road through Bütgenbach to seek secondary avenues farther south; three routes allocated to I SS Panzer Corps remained blocked, with others under fire. An attack farther north near Monschau failed abjectly when one German division arrived late to the battle and the other was knocked back. Only Peiper's foray showed clear promise in this sector. The 12th SS Panzer Division had been mauled, and other SS units seemed slow and clumsy.

The Americans, by contrast, demonstrated agility and a knack for concentrating firepower. Sixty thousand fresh troops had been shuttled into the Ardennes on Sunday, December 17, among the quarter million reinforcements who would arrive within a week. Four U.S. infantry divisions clotted the north shoulder so effectively that German army command's war diary acknowledged "the Elsenborn attack is gaining only quite insignificant ground," while the German Army Group B lamented "slower progress than anticipated." The tactical fortunes of Dietrich and his lieutenants seemed increasingly doubtful, to the point that Field Marshals Rundstedt and Model, watching the offensive come unstitched, agreed to abruptly shift the German main effort from the Sixth Panzer Army in the north to General Manteuffel's Fifth Panzer Army in the south. With northern routes denied or constricted, there was a new urgency on the German left, and the roads leading through Luxembourg toward Bastogne and then to the Meuse were now more vital than ever.

Reinforcements head to the front lines in the Ardennes.

German General Hasso
von Manteuffel

THE
SOUTH

THE OUR RIVER: "HOLD AT ALL COSTS"

ON SATURDAY MORNING, December 16, two of Man-teuffel's armored corps came down like wolves on a sheepfold, falling on an American regiment at an unnerving ratio of ten wolves for each sheep. Major General Norman "Dutch" Cota's 28th Infantry Division was holding an impossibly wide twenty-five-mile front along the Our River, with all three infantry regiments on the line. Instead of facing two German divisions across the river, as army intelligence had surmised, Cota's men found themselves fighting five, plus heavy enemy reinforcements.

As artillery and mortar barrages shredded field-phone wires and truck tires, German infiltrators forded the Our in swirling fog to creep up streambeds behind the American sen-tries. Forward outposts fell back, or perished, or surrendered.

"While I was being searched they came across my teeth [dentures] wrapped in a handkerchief in my pocket," a captured army engineer recorded. "These they kept." An American armored column rushing down a ridgetop road blundered into a German ambush: eleven light tanks were destroyed in as many minutes. From his command post in Wiltz, a brewing and tanning town ten miles west of the Our, Cota repeated orders from Major General Middleton at the VIII Corps headquarters in Bastogne, another ten miles farther west: "Hold at all costs." A soldier scribbled in his diary, "This place is not healthy anymore."

Yet, as in the north, frictions and vexations soon bedeviled the German attack. A bridge for the 2nd Panzer Division collapsed into the Our after only ten tanks had crossed. Engineers eventually built two spans stout enough to hold a Panther, at Gemünd and Dasburg, but steep, hairpin approach

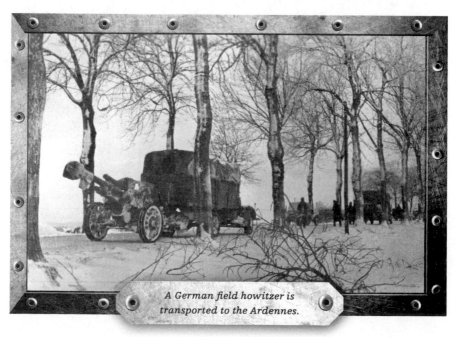

A German field howitzer is transported to the Ardennes.

roads, pitted by American artillery, reduced traffic to a crawl. Although Cota's flank regiments yielded ground in the face of flamethrowers and panzer fire, they imposed a severe penalty on the German timetable.

Along the American right, four German infantry divisions from the Seventh Army formed AUTUMN MIST's southern front. Over three days, the U.S. 109th Infantry Regiment would fall back slowly for four miles to Diekirch before joining forces with part of the 9th Armored Division. By Sunday night, the weight of metal and numbers won through for the Germans, but the American 112th Infantry Regiment withdrew in good order to the northwest, largely intact although now splintered away from the rest of the 28th Infantry Division. With Cota's permission, the regiment continued moving north to help defend the Belgian town of St.-Vith.

That left Cota a single regiment, the 110th Infantry, holding an eleven-mile front in the division center. Here Manteuffel swung his heaviest blow, with three divisions in XLVII Panzer Corps instructed to rip through to the city of Bastogne, specifically targeted for quick capture under a Führer order. By midday Sunday, the 110th was disintegrating, though not without a fight. In the medieval town of Clervaux, Luxembourg, one hundred GIs, including clerks and bakers, barricaded themselves inside a castle, firing from arrow slits in the tower at Germans in long leather coats scampering below. Wailing pleas for salvation rose from the dungeon, where dozens of women and children had taken refuge.

A mile up the road, in the three-story Hotel Claravallis, the flinty regimental commander, Colonel Hurley E. Fuller,

Clervaux Castle today

advised Cota by radio of his peril: at least a dozen panzers on the high ground firing into Clervaux; the castle besieged; ammunition short; artillery overrun or retreating. "Hold at all costs," Cota repeated. "No retreat. Nobody comes back."

At 7:30 on Sunday evening, Fuller was again on the radio to division headquarters, likening his predicament to the Alamo, when a staff officer rushed in to report enemy tanks on the street outside. "No more time to talk," Fuller told one of Cota's lieutenants, then slammed down the handset just before three shells demolished the hotel facade.

The castle, too, was burning. Flames danced from the tower roof, and black smoke stained the whitewashed inner walls. A final radio call went out Monday morning, December 18, before a panzer battered down the heavy wooden gates. At one P.M., the little garrison hoisted a white flag in surrender. Silence settled over Clervaux but for crackling fires and the shatter of glass from German looting. In a small inn that once housed the Red Cross club, a sign in the front window still proclaimed OF COURSE WE'RE OPEN.

Not far from Clervaux, frightened civilians in Diekirch wielded hammers and axes to demolish a huge sign erected in the fall to welcome the Americans, lest they be considered collaborators. On the heels of the retreating 109th Infantry Regiment, three thousand men, women, and children fled that Luxembourg town in bitter cold at midnight on Tuesday. The division command post pulled out Tuesday, first to Bastogne, then to Sibret, and eventually to Neufchâteau. A gaggle of army bandsmen, engineers, paymasters, and sawmill operators fought as a rear guard until overrun by whistle-blowing German paratroopers.

"This was the end," the official army history recorded. "Shots, blazing vehicles, and screaming wounded." Some GIs escaped by night in groups of ten with map scraps and radium-dial

A German armored personnel carrier (left) and a tank move to an assembly point.

compasses that glowed in the dark. Several hundred others were captured, including one young officer who described being propped up on a German staff car as a hood ornament, legs dangling over the grille, and driven east through march columns of German reinforcements who were "laughing at me as the trophy."

The 110th Infantry Regiment had been annihilated, with 2,500 battle casualties. Sixty American tanks had been reduced to smoking wreckage. Yet once again, space had been traded for time—the Germans had gained only a few miles and had spent forty-eight hours fighting for them. Once again, that bargain favored the defenders. The southern shoulder was jammed almost as effectively as the northern. The German Fifth Panzer Army now marched on Bastogne, true enough, but the stumbling, tardy advance by three bloodied divisions hardly resembled the victorious surprise attack of Hitler's fever dream.

German soldiers take offensive positions in the forest.

THE
CENTER

HOLDING ST.-VITH

ONLY IN THE CENTER of the German onslaught did AUTUMN MIST find particular success. Here many of the fourteen thousand green soldiers in the 106th Infantry Division sheltered in captured Siegfried Line pillboxes, as on Saturday, December 16, enemy spearheads to the left and right tried to envelop them in a pincer movement around the Schnee Eifel ridge on the German–Belgian border. Sixteen miles to the west lay St.-Vith. General Manteuffel hoped to capture the town within a day; the five main roads and three rail lines converging there were vital, given the hazards of moving cross-country through the Ardennes.

On no segment of the Western Front were GIs more outnumbered, yet sharp firefights that morning imperiled the German timetable here as elsewhere. After one enemy column was slapped around, a German soldier shouted, in English, "Take a ten-minute break. We'll be back." A GI answered, "We'll still be here."

But not for long. Here in this difficult terrain, about half of the 1,600 troopers in the 14th Cavalry Group under group commander Colonel Mark A. Devine, Jr., faced German paratroopers from the southern edge of the Sixth Panzer Army and Volksgrenadiers from the northern edge of the Fifth Panzer Army. The cavalry buckled. "Front lines still intact. Things well in hand," Devine reported from his command post in Manderfeld, but German shock troops were on the way. A final radio message—"Tanks seventy-five yards from command post. Firing direct fire. Out"—was followed by silence. At four o'clock on Saturday afternoon, after an enemy shell wounded a staff officer

American Sherman tanks in position outside of St.-Vith, Belgium.

and knocked Devine to the floor of his command post, he received permission from the 106th Infantry Division headquarters in St.-Vith to pull back two miles. Troopers put Manderfeld to the torch and retreated to the next ridgeline, blowing up eight of their dozen tank destroyers to keep them from being captured.

Devine's behavior now grew odd; perhaps he was suffering effects from the shell blast. Though there was little enemy pressure, he ordered his men to fall back farther, this time without authorization, eventually to seventeen miles from the original front.

But even a stalwart stand by the 14th Cavalry Group likely would not have long postponed the catastrophe that followed. With the American left flank abruptly unhinged, German paratroopers on Sunday had cantered through Manderfeld to Lanzerath, brushing sleeves with Colonel Peiper's SS column and further pressuring the 99th Infantry Division to the north as well as imperiling the 106th Infantry Division in the south.

In St.-Vith, Major General Alan Jones, a stocky native of Washington State, sought counsel from the VIII Corps commander, Major General Middleton. Except for an engineer battalion, virtually all division reserves had been hustled into the fight. Should the 106th's infantry regiments, entrenched along a twenty-eight-mile front, pull back?

U.S. Major General Troy H. Middleton, commander of VIII Corps

"You know how things are up there better than I do," Middleton said in a phone call from Bastogne. "But I agree it would be wise to withdraw them." In one of those mischances so common in war, a brief disruption on the line apparently kept Jones from hearing the second sentence. He hung up, telling his staff in St.-Vith, "Middleton says we should leave them in," even as Middleton told subordinates in Bastogne, "I just talked to Jones. I told him to pull his regiments off the Schnee Eifel." The 106th would stand pat, despite the howling enemy on both flanks. "He felt that he could hold," Middleton later observed. "He made a mistake. . . . He had a fighting heart."

Jones also believed that help was on the way, perhaps within hours. That optimism failed to account for the "indescribable confusion" of traffic "hurtling to the rear," in one major's description. "It was a case of every dog for himself . . . the most perfect traffic jam I have ever seen." Another officer conceded, "It wasn't orderly, it wasn't military, it wasn't a pretty sight." A tanker plowing against the exodus at one mile per hour reported that "the fear-crazed occupants of the vehicles fleeing to the rear had lost all reason."

By midday on Sunday, only the advance guard of replacements from Combat Command B of the 7th Armored Division had arrived in St.-Vith. The commander, a newly promoted brigadier general named Bruce C. Clarke, had been preparing to leave for Paris to undergo gallstone surgery when word came that "Alan Jones is having some trouble at St.-Vith." Clarke, a craggy engineer from upstate New York, found that Major General Jones's trouble included Germans

Sherman tank crews of the U.S. 3rd Armored Division wait for the command to enter combat.

on three sides, a disintegrating cavalry group, and fretful anxiety over his son, a lieutenant somewhere on the Schnee Eifel. Division staff officers stomped about, burning maps and flinging equipment into truck beds for evacuation. At one P.M., amid the chaos, Jones phoned Middleton again, telling the corps commander, "Things are looking up. . . . We are going to be all right." After ringing off, he told an astonished Clarke that Middleton had "enough troubles already" without worrying about the 106th Infantry Division.

The crackle of small-arms fire sent both generals hurrying to the third floor of the division command post in steep-roofed St. Josef's Kloster, where the devout had long cared for the sick, schooled the young, and bathed the bodies of the dead. Muzzle flashes twinkled along a bluff just east of town. "I've thrown in my last chips," Jones said, turning to Clarke. "I've got nothing left. You take it now." And with that, Major General Jones headed west to St.-Vith.

TRAPPED

JONES'S STAND-FAST decision not to withdraw had left two infantry regiments, the 422nd and 423rd, and five artillery battalions exposed to entrapment on the Schnee Eifel. On Sunday, the trap snapped shut when German columns from north and south converged in Schönberg, just across the Belgian border east of St.-Vith. By dusk, nine thousand GIs were surrounded on a bleak, snowy German moor. An icy west wind whipped through the fir trees, carrying the fateful whine of panzer engines. GIs huddling for warmth in foxholes listened impassively, displaying, one officer recorded, "absolutely no expression."

The Schnee Eifel did not provide sufficient coverage for men and machines.

*After an airdrop, medical supplies are dragged
to command centers.*

At 2:15 on Monday morning, a radio message from Major
General Jones at last ordered the two regiments to retreat toward Schönberg, where an armored spearhead from St.-Vith
would help them break out. Ammunition, food, and water for
the march were to be dropped by parachute. Colonel George L.
Descheneaux, commander of one of the regiments, bowed his
head. "My poor men," he said. "They'll be cut to pieces."

Cooks made towering stacks of pancakes, then destroyed
their kitchens. In dense fog at dawn, the retreat began, a
serpentine column of battalions trudging through the snow
while a parallel procession of trucks, jeeps, and towed artillery
bumped along cow paths and game trails. Men listened for
German V-weapons overhead and sought to follow the sound
westward. Even Descheneaux muttered, "Where the hell are

we?" Huge orange panels were readied to mark a supply drop zone, but no drop came. Bad weather and "command incoordination," as the Army Air Forces later termed the confusion, kept some planes grounded in England, while two dozen others shuttled emergency supplies between airfields in Belgium and France, futilely seeking information about the besieged regiments' location.

By midday, the Germans had found them, though Allied pilots could not. Artillery and mortar salvos fractured the columns, killing or wounding hundreds and scattering regiments, battalions, and companies across the plateau. Unsure where to shoot, given that enemy fire was falling from at least three directions, gunners began to spike their guns, driving in nails to disable them. With mortar ammunition gone and many riflemen reduced to just a few rounds, wet, cold, hungry troops crawled down ravines or sheltered among the trees and waited for dark. Another radio message from Major General Jones, now in Vielsalm, advised that no armored relief column was likely to appear. He added, "Attack Schönberg. Do maximum damage to enemy there. Then attack toward St.-Vith. This mission is of greatest importance to the nation. Good luck."

GIs wore as many layers as they could assemble to protect against the cold and wet.

At daybreak on Tuesday, December 19, three battalions from

A German Panzer IV with its commandant at the top, radio operator on the left, and gunner at the back.

the 422nd Infantry Regiment, quite lost but still game, moved out abreast, only to be lacerated by German tank and machine-gun fire. GIs again sought shelter, although not before unleashing a five-minute fusillade against shadowy figures in a nearby streambed, who proved to be comrades from the 423rd Infantry Regiment.

By one P.M., at least one battalion had been reduced to just fifty men from about three hundred. Relentless cannon fire sprayed the pastures between Radscheid and Auw. German loudspeakers bellowed promises of "showers, warm beds, and hotcakes." Spirits soared for a moment when a clanking Sherman appeared on the Schönberg road; then enemy crewmen inside the captured tank opened fire, and all hope perished.

At 2:30 P.M., with two thousand of his men now packed into a last-stand perimeter four hundred yards across, Colonel Descheneaux summoned his subordinates. "We're still sitting like fish in a pond," he told them. "I'm going to save as many men as I can, and I don't give a damn if I'm court-martialed." The order filtered through the ranks: "Destroy all weapons and equipment. We are about to surrender." As soldiers smashed their rifles against tree trunks and tossed the last ammunition clips into a creek, a major knotted together two white handkerchiefs and set off in search of parley. Descheneaux sat on the lip of a trench, weeping. Half a mile away, Colonel Charles Cavender, commander of the 423rd Infantry Regiment, had reached the same conclusion, giving

American POWs, who were captured during the first days of the surprise attack, are marched to the rear.

his troops thirty minutes to destroy all weapons and fling away any German souvenirs. An artillery officer stood on an ambulance waving a white snow cape, bellowing, "We surrender."

A few diehards lay low or scampered into the forest, but rank upon rank marched forward with hands raised. More than seven thousand would surrender, in the worst reverse for American arms in the war in Europe.

Long columns of prisoners plodded toward Germany, Jones's son among them, past wounded men wailing for help from the snowy fields. German reinforcements tramped by, pulling machine guns in wheelbarrows and catcalling about how panzers had already crossed the Meuse. In that gray tide making for St.-Vith, a captured gunner observed "tanks towing other tanks; tanks towing buses without engines; buses and trucks with red crosses all over them loaded down with ammo and troops."

"Do not flee," the German guards called out. "If you flee, you will be machine weaponed." Many GI prisoners had lost their overcoats and blankets, and at night they lay back to belly for warmth. Some chewed wax candles to ward off hunger, or wolfed down potato skins found in hog troughs. Through Rhineland towns they marched, pelted with stones and insults. "The Germans made us take off our overshoes and give them to the civilians," a squad leader from the 423rd Infantry Regiment wrote in his diary; in Koblenz, he added, a man in a business suit "hit me in the head with his briefcase. Guard said he was upset over recent bombing."

Among those transported by train into captivity was a twenty-two-year-old private first class named Kurt Vonnegut,

Jr., bound for a Dresden work camp. "Bayonets aren't much good against tanks," the future novelist wrote his family in Indiana.

> *The supermen marched us, without food, water or sleep to Limburg . . . where we were loaded and locked up, sixty men to each small, unventilated, unheated box car. . . . The floors were covered with fresh cow dung. . . . Half slept while the other half stood.*

More than a hundred miles east of the battle, at the Adlerhorst compound in the Taunus Hills, staff officers and headquarters clerks sorted through the latest reports on the Ardennes fighting. Given the disappointments on both flanks of his offensive, Hitler took heart at field dispatches from the Schnee Eifel. The Meuse, Antwerp, victory—all remained in play. To his generals the Führer proclaimed, "Success—complete success—is now in our grasp."

Führer Adolf Hitler, 1944

"ALL OF US, WITHOUT EXCEPTION, WERE ASTONISHED"

SHORTLY BEFORE three P.M. on Saturday, December 16, a SHAEF colonel tiptoed into Eisenhower's office in the Trianon Palace Hotel in Versailles, where General Omar Bradley and four others had just settled around a conference table with the supreme commander. The officer carried a sketchy dispatch from the front suggesting "strong and extensive attacks" in the Ardennes; an alarming number of German divisions already had been identified. Scrutinizing a map that showed blows against U.S. V and VIII Corps, Major General Strong, the SHAEF intelligence chief, wondered aloud if the enemy had designs on the Meuse and then Brussels. Beetle Smith indelicately recalled recent warnings to the 12th Army Group of resurgent strength in the German Sixth Panzer Army, but Bradley remained skeptical. This was likely nothing more than a spoiling attack, he said, intended to disrupt the Allied assault toward the Rhine; the rumpus would soon peter out. As the meeting broke up, Strong cautioned that "it would be wrong to underrate the Germans."

Eisenhower and Bradley dined that night at the supreme commander's handsome stone villa in St.-Germain-en-Laye. Despite sour tidings from the Ardennes, they were in a celebratory mood: word had just arrived from Washington of the president's decision to nominate Eisenhower for a fifth star. After spending sixteen years as a major, Eisenhower had ascended from lieutenant colonel to general of the U.S. Army in forty-five months. The two friends shared a bottle of champagne and played five rubbers of bridge.

Eisenhower, in a subsequent cable to Washington-based army chief of staff George Marshall, would confess that "all of us, without exception, were astonished" at the strength of AUTUMN MIST. Nearly a week would elapse until SHAEF

A German soldier examines a captured American heavy machine-gun vehicle.

intelligence confirmed the Germans' ambitions of creating a salient: splitting the Allied armies in half by moving forward to capture a long tongue of territory between the Allied troops in the north and south. The supreme commander sensed on the battle's first day that the trouble in the Ardennes went beyond a spoiling attack. Before repairing to St.-Germain for the evening, he had insisted that Bradley phone his headquarters to shift the 7th Armored Division to St.-Vith from the north, and the 10th Armored Division from the south toward Bastogne. When Bradley replied that Patton would resent the latter order, Eisenhower snapped, "Tell him that Ike is running this damn war."

Other moves quickly followed. SHAEF's only experienced combat reserve consisted of the 101st and 82nd Airborne Divisions; both had hoped for another month to recuperate from recent battles, but neither would get another day. Army tactical doctrine, learned in World War I, called for combating an enemy salient by first containing the intrusion from both sides. Paratroopers from the two divisions were ordered to the Ardennes immediately. The deployments of one armored division and three infantry divisions from Britain to the Continent would be accelerated, as would troopship sailings to France from the United States. Commanders at the front were told that Meuse bridges were to be held at all costs, or blown into the river if necessary. Patton also was instructed to prepare to swing north and to take Middleton's beleaguered VIII Corps under his wing. "By rushing out from his fixed defenses," Eisenhower added in an order to subordinates, "the enemy may give us the chance to turn his great gamble into his worst defeat." Supply dumps would be defended, evacuated, or burned as required, and defenses around newly liberated Paris strengthened.

In a message to Marshall, Eisenhower assured the chief that "in no quarter is there any tendency to place any blame upon Bradley"—he had "kept his head magnificently." Yet only grudgingly did Bradley acknowledge his peril. With the fighting front barely a dozen miles away, his room in the Hôtel Alfa was moved to the rear of the building as a precaution against stray artillery, and he now avoided the front door, entering through the kitchen. Aides removed the three-star insignia from his jeep and covered the stars on his helmet. During a brief moment of panic, staff officers buried secret documents in the headquarters courtyard, disguising the cache as a grave and marking it with a wooden cross and dog tags.

Still, Bradley affected nonchalance. Logisticians and engineers were told to continue working on the army group's plan to cross the Rhine River into Germany. After supper on Monday, December 18, upon studying a map that showed at least four U.S. divisions retreating westward and others threatened with encirclement, he told an aide, "I don't take too serious a view of it, although the others will not agree with me."

Among those who no longer agreed was First Army commander Courtney Hodges. At his headquarters at the Hôtel Britannique in the city of Spa, Belgium, he had shared Bradley's defiant attitude of denial for more than a day after the German attack began. Fourteen of his First Army divisions were holding a 165-mile front from Aachen, Germany, to Luxembourg. But as Sunday wore on, deep unease began spreading through his command post. Church bells pealed to signal a civilian curfew from six P.M. to seven A.M. Mortar crews outside Spa scattered tin pans and crockery around their pits as makeshift alarms against infiltrators. Birds were mistaken for German paratroopers, and improvised patrols scrambled off in pursuit. "Thermite grenades were issued with which we could destroy our papers," Forrest Pogue informed his diary.

On December 18, Hodges ordered the evacuation of military and civilians. Reports put German panzers first at six miles, then two miles from Spa. Both sightings proved false, but they accelerated the evacuation. "I imagine that the Germans felt like [this] when they had to leave Paris," Pogue wrote. Belgian schoolchildren assembled to sing "The Star-Spangled Banner" while their parents ripped down American flags and photos of President Roosevelt. Twelve hundred patients and medicos emptied the 4th Convalescent Hospital within ninety minutes, bolting for Huy. German V-1s hit two fleeing convoys, killing two dozen GIs and leaving charred truck chassis scattered across the road.

Monday night at ten P.M., the command group pulled out for

Lieutenant General Courtney Hodges, commander of the U.S. First Army

A German Luftwaffe Heinkel bomber

Chaudfontaine, near Liège, where a new headquarters opened at midnight in the Hôtel des Bains. Left behind in Spa were secret maps and food simmering on the stove.

EVACUATION of the vast supply dumps in eastern Belgium seemed far more ambitious than the abandonment of a headquarters hotel, but the task was capably done. Some stockpiles were beyond either removal or destruction—for instance, the eight million rations stored around Liège. Quartermasters in Paris also calculated that even if the biggest depots along the Meuse were captured, enough stocks could be found in the rear to last ten days or more, until emergency shipments arrived from the United States. But smaller supply depots, hospitals, and repair shops were ordered to move west of the river. With help from 1,700 First

Army trucks and 2,400 railcars, about 45,000 tons of matériel and 50,000 vehicles were shifted out of harm's way, along with a quarter million rear-echelon soldiers who were mainly administrators and patients.

Three miles of explosive cord was used to blow up stored grenades, mines, and torpedoes—as well as twenty tons of sugar, rice, and flour—in an exposed supply dump near Malmédy. Most critical were the 3.5 million gallons of gasoline, largely in five-gallon cans grouped in thousand-can stacks, now within ten miles of Lieutenant Colonel Peiper's SS spearhead. The fuel dump covered several square miles of woodland near Stavelot. In all, 800,000 gallons of gas and 300,000 gallons of vehicle grease and oil were spirited away beginning Sunday night, as Peiper approached the town; another 134,000 gallons were ignited as a flaming roadblock on Highway N-28. More than two million additional gallons were quickly evacuated from Spa using ten-ton tractor-trailers and railcars rushed to a nearby siding. Except for several minor caches captured by the Germans, Rundstedt's tanks and trucks would be forced to rely on their own dwindling fuel stocks.

THE LAST GERMAN AIRBORNE OPERATION

BIRDS MIGHT HAVE been mistaken for German parachutists near Spa, but more than a thousand actual German airborne troops were due to be dropped north of Malmédy on Zero Day to further disrupt American defenses.

Nothing went right for the enemy. Half the pilots had never flown in combat, and many paratroopers either were novices or had not jumped since the attack on Holland in 1940. "Don't be afraid. Be assured that I will meet you personally by 1700 [5 P.M.] on the first day," General Dietrich had told the mission commander, Colonel Friedrich von der Heydte. After confusion and blunders delayed the jump for a day, a howling crosswind on Sunday morning scattered paratroopers up to fifty kilometers from the drop zone. Two hundred jumpers were mistakenly dropped near Bonn, and American gunners shot down several planes. With a single mortar, little ammunition, and no functioning radios, von der Heydte rounded up three hundred men, who stumbled into a losing firefight before fleeing in small groups; the colonel surrendered after briefly hiding outside Monschau. Two-thirds of the original thousand were killed or captured. That was the end of what proved to be the last German airborne operation of the war.

A patrol of U.S. infantry searches the woods near a known German parachutists' drop.

SOWING HYSTERIA ACROSS THE WESTERN FRONT

ANOTHER GERMAN IDEA, Operation GREIF, or CONDOR, proved no more competent. Under the flamboyant Viennese commando officer Otto Skorzeny, 2,000 men had been recruited into the 150th Armored Brigade for behind-the-lines sabotage, reconnaissance, and havoc. Their motor fleet included a dozen Panthers modified to resemble U.S. Sherman tanks, German Fords painted Allied olive drab, and a small fleet of captured U.S. Army trucks, jeeps, and scout cars. About 150 men who spoke English would lead raiding parties to seize three Meuse bridges. They were issued captured or counterfeit identification documents, as well as GI uniforms, many of which had been taken from American prisoners under the pretext of disinfection. To mimic American cigarette-smoking techniques and other mannerisms, the men studied the famous actor Humphrey Bogart in the movie *Casablanca*.

All for naught. The Sixth Panzer Army's troubles on the

north shoulder disrupted Skorzeny's timetable, and a set of GREIF orders discovered on a dead German officer alerted the Americans to the deception. On Monday, December 18, First Army military police stopped three men in a jeep near Aywaille who were unable to give the day's password; a search revealed German pay books and grenades. Four others on a Meuse bridge in Liège included a GI imposter who carried the identification card of a captain but the dog tags of a private. He and his comrades were found to be wearing swastika armbands beneath their army field jackets. In all, sixteen infiltrators were swiftly captured in American uniforms, and an additional thirty-five were killed without effecting a single act of sabotage on the Meuse. Most of Skorzeny's brigade eventually returned to the regular German infantry and were sent into battle near Malmédy, where inexperience and a lack of artillery led to heavy casualties. Skorzeny himself suffered a nasty head wound.

The sole accomplishment of GREIF was to sow hysteria across the Western Front. A talkative, imaginative German lieutenant captured in Liège claimed to be part of a team sent to kill Eisenhower. Colonel Skorzeny, he said, had already infiltrated American lines with 60 assassins. Rumor quickly increased the number to 150. It was said that some infiltrators carried vials of

Captured German soldiers trained by Otto Skorzeny had pretended to be Americans.

sulfuric acid to fling in the faces of suspicious sentries, that many spoke English better than any GI, that they recognized one another by rapping their helmets twice, or by wearing blue scarves, or by leaving unfastened the top button of a uniform shirt. It was said that some might be costumed as priests, nuns, or barkeeps.

Military police at checkpoints sought to distinguish native English speakers from frauds by testing their pronunciation of various words, including *wreath, writhe, wealth, rather,* and *with nothing.* Some asked the identity of the Windy City, since an intelligence report advised that "few Germans can pronounce Chicago correctly." Other questions included: What is the price of an airmail stamp? What is Sinatra's first name? Who is Mickey Mouse's girlfriend? Where is Little Rock? The American photographer Robert Capa, who had a Hungarian accent, was arrested for failing to know the capital of Nebraska. The military historian Forrest Pogue, when asked the statehouse location in his native Kentucky, carefully replied, "The capital is Frankfort, but you may think it is Louisville."

With Skorzeny and his assassins presumed to be still at large, Eisenhower reluctantly agreed to move from his villa in the Paris suburb of St.-Germain to smaller quarters nearer his office in the Trianon Palace Hotel in Versailles. Each day his black limousine continued to follow the usual route to and from SHAEF, but with the rear seat occupied by a lieutenant colonel named Baldwin B. Smith, whose broad shoulders, prominent head, and impatient appearance made him a perfect body double for the supreme commander.

A CRUCIAL MEETING IN VERDUN

Generals Patton, Eisenhower, and Bradley meet in Bastogne, Belgium.

DECEMBER 19, 1944

THE REAL EISENHOWER, traveling in a bulletproof Cadillac, arrived in Verdun, France, for a war council on Tuesday morning, December 19. At an ancient French army barracks within a muddy quadrangle, he soon was joined by U.S. Generals Bradley and Devers, as well as Patton, who drove up smoking a cigar in a jeep with plexiglass doors and a .30-caliber machine gun mounted on the hood. At 11:30 A.M., they climbed upstairs to a dank stone squad room with a single potbellied stove, a large table, and a map unfurled across a wall.

"The present situation is to be regarded as one of opportunity for us and not of disaster," Eisenhower said, settling into his chair. "There will be only cheerful faces at this conference table."

Two staff officers reviewed the battlefront in detail. At least seventeen German divisions had joined the attack already; the identities of most were known. The heaviest pressure could be felt at St.-Vith and Bastogne, two vital road centers. Atrocities had been documented. Daily Luftwaffe sorties over St.-Vith had declined sharply from six hundred on Sunday, although a persistent overcast sky had grounded Allied planes also. Seven French infantry battalions would help defend the Meuse, along with half a dozen regiments moved forward from the Communication Zone to support troops at the front. American strength in the Ardennes had doubled since Saturday, to about 180,000 troops in ten infantry and three armored divisions. More would soon follow.

Eisenhower then spoke. Devers's 6th Army Group would assume the defensive in Alsace, in the northeast corner of France bordering Germany, he said, and contribute reserves for the Ardennes farther north. Scattered forces must be pulled together for "positive concerted action." Holding the high ground south of Liège would keep supply depots outside enemy artillery range. By squeezing the German salient, shoring up defense of the bridges over the Meuse, blunting the enemy advance, and creating "a supply desert," they could smash Rundstedt's bulge—as it was now called—with an American counterblow again aimed at the Rhine River. George Patton's U.S. Third Army, which currently held an eighty-mile front with three corps facing the Saar River, would pivot north to knife into the exposed German left flank.

Peering down the long table at Patton, Eisenhower asked in his booming voice, "George, how soon can you get an attack off?"

"On December twenty-second," Patton replied, "with three divisions."

Leaning forward, Eisenhower quickly calculated distance, time, and the number of troops. He was asking Patton to move more than thirty thousand soldiers almost one hundred miles over winter roads. "I'd even settle for the twenty-third if it takes that long to get three full divisions," Eisenhower conceded.

Eisenhower declined Bradley's invitation to stay for lunch; he would eat a sandwich in his car on the way back to Versailles. Turning to Patton before getting into the car, Eisenhower said, "George, every time I get promoted, I get attacked."

Patton chuckled. "Yes, and every time you get attacked, I bail you out."

Lieutenant General George Patton in an open-air jeep at the front.

A LINE ON THE MAP

Field Marshal Bernard Montgomery, commander of the 21st Army Group

EISENHOWER HAD URGED his generals in Verdun "to avoid any discouragement or feeling of disappointment in the changed situation." However, a new development left Omar Bradley not only discouraged and disappointed but also furious.

Bernard Montgomery made it clear to SHAEF's deputy operations officer, Major General John Whiteley, "that Ike ought to place me in operational command of all troops on the northern half of the front. I consider he should be given a direct order by someone to do so." Back in Versailles, British Major General Strong agreed that the Ardennes battlefield would best be managed by two commanders—Montgomery in the north and Bradley in the south—rather than by Bradley's 12th Army Group alone. The decision was driven by the news from British intelligence on Tuesday evening that the road to Namur was vulnerable and that if German shock troops crossed the Meuse there, they could reach Brussels within hours.

Rousted from his bed by Whiteley and Strong on Tuesday night, Beetle Smith, the chief of staff, listened to their proposal to expand Montgomery's role. He also heard their warnings of "further deterioration" at the front caused by Bradley's distance from his armies on the ground. Bradley's headquarters was in Luxembourg City, and neither he nor his ranking officers had yet visited the front. But then Smith rounded in anger on the staff officers. Clearly these two Britishmen did not consider the Yanks capable of handling the crisis, Smith charged. Where did their loyalties lie?

As Whiteley and Strong slunk away in the face of this tirade, Smith phoned Eisenhower, finding the supreme commander still in his office at eleven P.M. Fuming, Smith described the

The people of Brussels give British and Belgian troops a hearty welcome when the city was first liberated in September 1944.

proposal while grudgingly conceding that it had merit: among other benefits, Montgomery would more likely commit British reserves to the battle if he commanded them. Eisenhower, staring at a huge wall map, promptly agreed. With a grease pencil, he drew a line on the map from Givet on the Meuse east through the Ardennes to Prüm in Germany. St.-Vith fell north of the line, Bastogne south.

While the supreme commander pondered this demarcation, Smith phoned Bradley in Luxembourg City.

Ike thinks it may be a good idea to turn over to Monty your two armies in the north and let him run that side of the bulge from 21st Group. . . . It seems the logical thing to do. Monty can take care of everything north of the bulge and you'll have everything south.

General Omar Bradley, commander of the 12th Army Group

Bradley answered cautiously. He noted that no hint of this scheme had arisen in Verdun that morning. Although three enemy armies were now positioned between his command post and the bulk of his army group to the north, he considered his communication difficulties insignificant. "I'd question whether such a changeover is necessary," he added.

By Wednesday morning, when Eisenhower called personally to

confirm the reconfiguration, Bradley had worked himself into a seething temper. "By God, Ike, I cannot be responsible to the American people if you do this. I resign." Major General Strong, listening to the phone conversation in Eisenhower's office, watched a deep flush creep up the supreme commander's neck.

"Brad, I—not you—am responsible to the American people. Your resignation therefore means absolutely nothing."

The British Chief of Staff Sir Alan Brooke in France, previously Commanding General of the Second Corps of England.

Bradley continued to protest, if in a lower key, until Eisenhower ended the conversation: "Well, Brad, those are my orders." He then phoned Montgomery at his command post in Zonhoven, Belgium. "We've now got two battles, two separate battles," Eisenhower said, bellowing into the receiver. "I think you'd better take charge of the northern one, and leave Bradley to deal with the southern one."

At 12:52 P.M., a SHAEF log entry confirmed that "Field Marshal Montgomery has been placed in charge of the northern flank." He would command the U.S. First and Ninth Armies, as well as his own army group; Bradley's 12th Army Group was left with only Patton's Third Army. An officer in Bradley's headquarters reported that he was "absolutely livid. Walked up and down and cursed Monty."

The field marshal relished his new orders. He arrived at Courtney Hodges's headquarters at 1:30 on Wednesday. Three hours later, the British and the Americans had a plan. First Army would dig in where it could and, with help from U.S. Lieutenant General William Simpson's Ninth Army, assemble a strike force to counterattack the Germans from the north, complementing Patton's blow from the south. British Lieutenant General Miles Dempsey's Second Army would continue to feed forces down from Holland, and British supplies would reinforce U.S. losses to the tune of 100 twenty-five-pounder

A U.S. transport and supply column moves through the Ardennes Forest.

guns with 300,000 rounds of ammunition, 20,000 snowsuits, 2,000 trip flares, and 350 Sherman tanks fitted with cleats for better traction. By nine o'clock that evening, all Meuse bridges would be rigged for demolition.

SHAEF ordered the new command arrangement to remain secret. Censorship, already tightened to prevent full disclosure of the AUTUMN MIST reverses, also

Crossing a Meuse bridge in September 1944.

ensured that Americans at home would be spared knowing that much of the U.S. Army in Europe now was led by a short Brit in a black beret. "They seemed delighted to have someone to give them orders," Montgomery told Field Marshal Alan Brooke, with some justification. Brooke warned him not to gloat, but the field marshal could not help himself. "The Americans have taken a 1st Class bloody nose," he wrote a friend in London. "I am busy sorting out the mess."

As for Bradley, Eisenhower proposed awarding him a Bronze Star as a conciliation for losing two-thirds of his command. He also asked George Marshall to consider giving Bradley a fourth star. "I retain all my former confidence in him," Eisenhower wrote the chief. "It would have a fine effect generally."

IN THE RAW

Refugees flee Bastogne with their animals and possessions.

Watching for the enemy near Lutrebois, Belgium,
January 1, 1945.

BASTOGNE:
THE LEFT FLANK

CIVILIAN REFUGEES with woeful tales of burning villages and Germans in close pursuit tumbled into Bastogne, "an ancient town in the dreariest part of the Ardennes," as a Belgian guidebook had once described it. Carts piled high with furniture and scuffed baggage clogged the main square, despite army placards warning that UNATTENDED VEHICLES WILL BE IMPOUNDED BY MILITARY POLICE. Shops along the Grand-Rue pulled tight their shutters after the power failed on Sunday, and by midday on Monday, December 18, the grumble of artillery could be heard even in the cellar corridors of the Sisters of Notre Dame, a boarding school where hundreds took refuge.

The first paratroopers from the U.S. 101st Airborne Division arrived at dusk on Monday after a

In winter camouflage, the 82nd Airborne
Division pushes through the snow.

sleet-spattered hundred-mile drive from Reims, France. Under Major General Matthew Ridgway, XVIII Airborne Corps had been directed to help seal the twenty-mile gap between V Corps and VIII Corps, with Brigadier General James M. Gavin's 82nd Airborne Division making for Werbomont, southwest of Spa, and the 101st bound for Bastogne. Sergeants had trotted through the troop barracks the previous night, bawling, "Get out of the sack. You ain't reserve no more," and officers interrupted a ballet performance to order paratroopers in the audience to assemble for battle.

Since November, the 101st had been plagued with several dozen AWOL incidents each week, as well as the usual drunken brawls; troopers held contests to see who could punch out the most windows in Reims. Worse yet, many of the division's senior leaders were absent. They included the commander,

Major General Maxwell D. Taylor, who had flown to Washington; his assistant commander, who was in England with seventeen officers; and the chief of staff, who had killed himself with a pistol a week earlier. That left command to the division artillery chief, a short, genial brigadier general from Washington, D.C., named Anthony Clement McAuliffe. Having graduated from West Point at the end of World War I, McAuliffe had risen slowly through the ranks of the peacetime army as a gunner with an interest in both technological and sociological innovation. Before joining the 101st, he had worked on development of the jeep and the bazooka, and on a study of race relations in the service. He had parachuted into Normandy and landed by glider in Holland; now he drove to Bastogne at the head of a division he led by default.

On January 16, 1945, American ambulances and other vehicles arrive in the destroyed town of Foy, Belgium.

Several thousand replacement troopers who had received barely a week of field training jammed into open cattle trucks behind him—"like olives in a jar," as one account noted. Some, without helmets or rifles, pleaded for both from the retreating GIs who clogged every road west of Bastogne. COMZ (the acronym for the Communication Zone, whence movements and supplies were organized) dispatched an emergency convoy hauling five thousand entrenching shovels, two thousand sets of wool underwear, and five thousand pairs of arctic overshoes,

Narrow roads made movement difficult in the Ardennes.

sizes 6 to 14. Through Monday night and early the next morning, twelve thousand cold, soaking-wet paratroopers and glidermen poured into Bastogne. By ten A.M. on Tuesday, all four regiments had arrived, accompanied by a few disoriented artillery and armor units grabbed along the way. Brigadier General McAuliffe put his command post in the Hôtel de Commerce, facing the train station, and his first wounded into a local seminary.

Bearing down on Bastogne were three divisions from Germany's Fifth Panzer Army, well aware of U.S. reinforcements thanks to careless American radio chatter. Little in this stage of the battle had unfolded according to the German master plan. Fuel shortages pinched harder with each passing hour. Panzer tracks chewed up roads so severely that wheeled vehicles by the score were abandoned in mud trenches. With few engineers to clear mines, tank crews took up the task with rake-like harrows and rollers found in farm sheds. Foot soldiers slouching westward almost outpaced Manteuffel's motorized columns, and Field Marshal Model now privately doubted that AUTUMN MIST could achieve even the modest goals of the so-called small solution, much less the seizure of the port of Antwerp.

Bastogne and its seven radial roads assumed ever greater importance to the Germans, and spearhead troops smashed into the feeble roadblocks east of town, setting U.S. half-tracks ablaze, then picking off GIs silhouetted against the flames. Forty Sherman tanks were demolished in a single night, and defenders in nearby Neffe retreated under showers

German Tiger (front) and Panther (rear) tanks assemble.

of incendiary grenades. "We're not driven out," one officer radioed, "but burned out." Under the steady onslaught of those three German divisions—2nd Panzer, 26th Volksgrenadier, and Panzer Lehr—the American defenses buckled and bent.

But they did not break. The gunfight cost the Germans four precious hours of daylight on Tuesday. Farther north on the same day, U.S. combat engineers dynamited culverts and bridges, and felled trees with such obstructive skill that frustrated German LVIII Corps countermarched up various blind alleys in search of easier routes west.

No less vital in delaying the enemy was Middleton's order that the 10th Armored Division defend a trio of strongpoints outside Bastogne. An especially vicious brawl unfolded in

Noville, a foggy sinkhole four miles north of town, where fifteen Sherman tanks and other armor arrived in time to confront much of the 2nd Panzer Division. A murky dawn on Tuesday brought the telltale rattle of German tanks, followed by vague gray shapes drifting from the east. The Americans answered with artillery—aimed "by guess and by God" because of map shortages—and even pistol fire. Soon the fog lifted like a curtain to reveal German armor and grenadiers spread thickly across a slope half a mile distant. American tank destroyers ripped into nine panzers, leaving three in flames. German infantrymen turned and fled, pursued by bullets.

A U.S. soldier fires a howitzer.

All morning and through the afternoon, the battle raged. A battalion of 101st paratroopers from Bastogne attacked on a dead run at two P.M., colliding with another German assault just beginning to boil across a smoky ridgeline. Enemy barrages pounded Noville to rubble, killing the paratrooper commander; only artillery counterfire kept grenadiers on three sides from overrunning the Americans.

At midday on Wednesday, December 20, a radio message to the Hôtel de Commerce advised, "All reserves committed. Situation critical." McAuliffe authorized survivors to fall back into Bastogne at five P.M., cloaked in smoke and darkness; for want of a tank crew, paratroopers drove one of the four remaining Shermans. American casualties exceeded four hundred men, but the 2nd Panzer Division had lost over six

American soldiers in winter camouflage on patrol near Bastogne.

U.S. Army Signal Corps photographers and cameramen document German POWs.

hundred, plus thirty-one panzers and at least two days' time in the German drive toward the Meuse.

Strongpoints east of Bastogne, now reinforced by the 501st Parachute Infantry Regiment, proved just as formidable for the German Panzer Lehr and 26th Volksgrenadier Divisions. Barbed wire and musketry near Neffe snared German troops in what paratroopers called a "giant mantrap." "We took no prisoners," a captain reported. "We mowed them down as if they were weeds." Renewed enemy attacks on Wednesday ran into "a dam of fire" laid by guns firing from Bastogne.

Little profit had been found in frontal assaults, and belatedly the Germans revised their tactics. General Manteuffel urged his 2nd Panzer Division to press westward past the Our River despite gasoline shortages so severe that the division wasted a day waiting for fuel trucks. The Panzer Lehr

Division would leave a regiment to besiege Bastogne with the 26th Volksgrenadier Division, but most of the division now turned left to bypass the town on the south.

Among the few heartening reports to reach the Fifth Panzer Army on Wednesday was the annihilation of a 101st Airborne Division medical detachment, which had failed to post sentries at a crossroads encampment west of Bastogne. Shortly before midnight, a German patrol of six panzers and half-tracks raked the medical tents and trucks with gunfire. Within minutes, the division surgeon had been captured, along with ten other medical officers and more than a hundred enlisted men, as well as stretchers, wounded patients, surgical instruments, and penicillin.

"Above all," Middleton had instructed McAuliffe, "don't get yourself surrounded." Precisely how eighteen thousand Americans, under orders to hold Bastogne at all costs against forty-five thousand Germans, should avoid encirclement was not clear, particularly in weather so dismal that Allied aircraft flew a total of twenty-nine sorties in Europe on Wednesday, only nine of them over the Ardennes. A day later, on Thursday morning, December 21, an enemy column severed the last open road south, and Bastogne was indeed cut off. Resurgent optimism flared through the German chain of command.

"NUTS"

AT 11:30 on Friday morning, a delegation of four Germans carrying a white flag appeared in a grove of spruce trees dusted with new snow southwest of Bastogne. "We are *parliamentaires*," an English-speaking captain told an American officer, then presented a note composed on a captured American typewriter, with each umlaut inserted by hand, and addressed *an den amerikanischen Kommandeur der eingeschlossen Stadt Bastogne*, "to the American commander of the surrounded city of Bastogne." An appended translation explained:

> *The fortune of war is changing. . . . There is only one possibility to save the encircled U.S.A. troops from total annihilation: In order to think it over, a term of two hours will be granted beginning with the presentation of this note. If this proposal should be rejected, one*

German artillery corps and six heavy AA battalions
are ready to annihilate. . . . All the serious civilian losses
caused by this artillery fire would not correspond with
the well-known American humanity.

The note had been authorized by Lieutenant General Heinrich von Lüttwitz, commander of XLVII Panzer Corps.

At 12:25 P.M., the ultimatum reached McAuliffe in his smoke-stained command post, which reeked of cordite from a bombing raid the previous night. Encircled or not, the 101st remained almost at full strength; only five battalions among the four regiments had so far seen intense combat. Six hundred stragglers, mostly from the 28th Infantry Division, had been fed a hot meal and mustered into Team Snafu, a quick-reaction battalion. The Bastogne arsenal included forty Shermans; armor officers mimeographed useful tips on tank tactics for their infantry brethren. Six artillery battalions were arranged in circular gun pits to allow each battery to shoot at every compass point, although McAuliffe, a field artilleryman for a quarter century, had advised his cannoneers not to fire "until you see the whites of their eyes." Vehicles were slathered with whitewash for camouflage, and Belgian linen closets provided sheets for snow capes. The men now received only two meals a day, but cooks had whipped up excellent pancakes from doughnut flour discovered in a Red Cross pantry.

Perhaps inspired by the legendary epithet uttered by a French general when asked to surrender at Waterloo— "*Merde!*"—McAuliffe offered a one-word answer to the ultimatum: "Nuts." A paratrooper officer then handed it to the

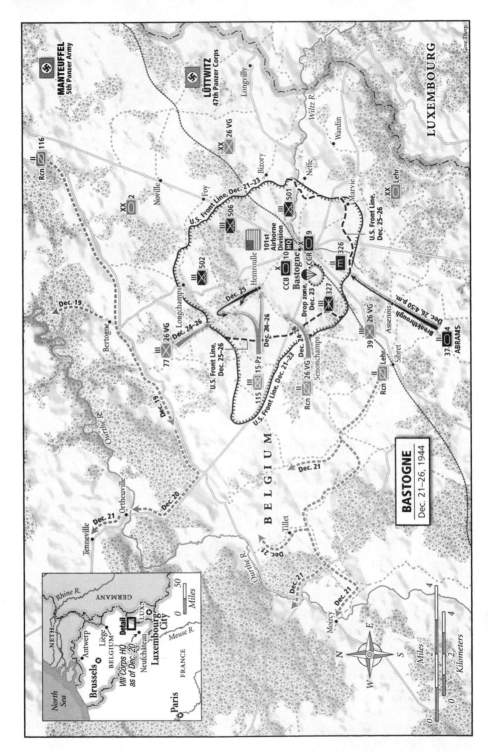

MANTEUFFEL
5th Panzer Army

LÜTTWITZ
47th Panzer Corps

LUXEMBOURG

Gene Thorp

Rcn 116

Longuyon

Wiltz R.

Wardin

26 VG

Noville

Foy

Bizory

Nefie

Marvie

2

U.S. Front Line, Dec. 21–23

501

U.S. Front Line, Dec. 25–26

Lehr

506

U.S. Front Line, Dec. 25–26

502

Hemroulle

101st
Airborne
Division

CCB

10 HQ

X CCR

9

326

Dec. 25

Bastogne

Drop zone,
Dec. 23

Breakthrough Dec. 26, 4:50 p.m.

Dec. 19

Bertogne

Longchamps

Dec. 24–26

Dec. 24–26

327

39

26 VG

Assenois

37 4
ABRAMS

26 VG

77

Sibret

Lehr

U.S. Front Line,
Dec. 25–26

15 Pz

Dec. 21–23

Senonchamps

Dec. 19

115

U.S. Front Line, Dec. 21–23

26 VG

Rcn

Rcn Lehr

Ourthe R.

Ortheuville

Dec. 20

Dec. 21

Tenneville

Dec. 21

Tillet

Ourthe R.

Dec. 21

B E L G I U M

Dec. 21

Moircy

Dec. 21

BASTOGNE
Dec. 21–26, 1944

N
W   E
S

Miles
0   2   4

Kilometers
0   4

North
Sea

NETH.

Rhine R.

GERMANY

Antwerp

Liège

Brussels

BELGIUM

Detail

LUX.
Luxembourg
City

Neufchâteau

VIII Corps HQ
as of Dec. 20

Meuse R.

FRANCE

Paris

Miles
0   50

Map legend is on page vii.

Brigadier General Anthony McAuliffe, commander of the 101st Airborne Division

"*parliamentaires,*" whereupon a baffled German officer asked, "Is the reply negative or affirmative?"

"The reply is decidedly *not* affirmative," the American said. "If you don't understand what 'nuts' means, in plain English, it is the same as 'go to hell.' . . . We will kill every goddamn German that tries to break into this city."

"We will kill many Americans. This is war," the German officer replied.

Only after the event did an irate Manteuffel learn of Lüttwitz's gamble. "This is crazy," he told the corps commander. "Now we must find the artillery and bomber force to make good your threat and level the town."

ST.-VITH: THE RIGHT FLANK

AS BASTOGNE WAS a poisonous thorn in General Manteuffel's left flank, St.-Vith was a prickly nettle on his right. Now the easternmost U.S.-held town of any size in the Ardennes, St.-Vith had over the past three days become a breakwater, with a "German tide rushing past on the north and south and rising against its eastern face," in the description of the army official history.

The town had been named for Saint Vitus, a Sicilian child martyr. Various unpleasantries had befallen St.-Vith since its founding in the twelfth century, but none was uglier than the battle that engulfed the town in December 1944.

The German troops approaching the town had all but destroyed the 106th Infantry Division on the Schnee Eifel, but the German plan to occupy St.-Vith by six P.M. on December 17 fell short. General Manteuffel's frustration grew day by day.

The Allied troops included the 7th Armored Division now

The 7th Armored Division advances through Belgium.

under Brigadier General Bruce Clarke, following Major General Jones's flight west, and Major General Ridgway's XVIII Airborne Corps.

Gunfights had erupted around the town on December 18 and 19, but German lunges were thrown back. With supply lines cut, howitzers were limited to seven rounds per gun each day. Gunners rummaged for ammunition in abandoned dumps; some batteries reported firing "old propaganda shells just to keep projectiles whistling around German ears." Riflemen were told on December 20 that "for every round fired, a corpse must hit the ground." In St.-Vith's narrow streets, broken glass crunched beneath the hooves of cattle fleeing a burning slaughterhouse. Smoke blackened the faces and uniforms of soldiers trying to stay warm over fires lit in tins filled with gasoline-soaked sand. One soldier later described mounting a local counterattack with a "cold, plodding, unwilling, ragged double line plunging up to their knees in snow."

On Wednesday, December 20, Manteuffel ordered two Volksgrenadier divisions to finish off the town, supported by SS tanks. The next day, German artillery tore into American trenches as waves of infantry swept through the dense woods and Panthers fired flat-trajectory flares to blind Sherman crews. Half an hour later, Clarke's line had been punctured in three places. At ten P.M., he ordered his troops to fall back onto

Surveillance from a muddy foxhole.

German troops with ice frozen to their eyebrows.

high ground a kilometer west of town, but by then, nearly a thousand GIs had been killed or captured, and twenty thousand others remained vulnerable in a shrinking defended area east of the Salm River.

Ridgway now struggled to control a front that abruptly increased in width from twenty-five miles to eighty-five. If the 101st Airborne Division could continue to fight effectively while surrounded, Ridgway wondered why a comparable combat force in the Salm salient could not do the same. But by early Friday, December 22, that force showed signs of disintegration. Patrols simply vanished; an entire battalion staff at Neubrück, three miles south of St.-Vith, had been killed or captured. Clarke reported that his combat command had lost half its strength.

"This terrain is not worth a nickel an acre," Clarke added, and urged withdrawal. The 7th Armored Division commander, Brigadier General Robert W. Hasbrouck, now encamped at Vielsalm, twelve miles west of St.-Vith, warned that fuel and ammunition shortages had become dire. Just after eleven A.M., Hasbrouck told Ridgway in a message, "If we don't get out of here . . . before night, we will not have a 7th Armored Division left." To his old friend Brigadier General

Clearing snow from an antitank gun.

William M. Hoge, whose combat command in the 9th Armored Division also faced dismemberment, Ridgway said, "We're not going to leave you in here to be chopped to pieces. . . . We're going to get you out of here." Hoge replied plaintively, "How can you?"

In midafternoon on Friday, Ridgway reluctantly ordered Hasbrouck to withdraw all U.S. forces across the Salm River. Montgomery, who had watched the St.-Vith drama with mounting anxiety, rejoiced. "They can come back with all honor," he said. "They put up a wonderful show."

Fourteen hours of December darkness and a cold snap that froze the mud on Friday night allowed most to escape, narrowly averting a catastrophe even worse than the Schnee Eifel surrender. A radio dispatch to a field commander instructed, "Your orders are: Go west. Go west. Go west." GIs urinated on frozen M-1 rifle bolts to free them, then tramped single file on forest trails and farm tracks, each man gripping the belt or pack straps of the colleague ahead. Others tried to be invisible by clinging to tank hulls lit up by scorching enemy tracers. German artillery searched roads and junctions, and only the late arrival of a ninety-truck American convoy lugging five thousand shells permitted counterfire by gunners west of the Salm. "Wrapped in scarves and mufflers, only their eyes showing," as one lieutenant wrote, retreating troops made for the bridges at Salmchâteau and Vielsalm; Hasbrouck stood on a road shoulder to welcome his men to safety. An 82nd Airborne Division trooper south of Werbomont called to a passing column, "What the hell you guys running from? We been here two days and ain't seen a German yet." A weary

American soldiers advance, attempting to surround German troops during the battle for Bastogne.

voice replied, "Stay right where you are, buddy. In a little while you won't even have to look for 'em."

Ridgway estimated that fifteen thousand troops and one hundred tanks escaped. As many tanks were lost, and casualties east of the Salm approached five thousand, more than the losses incurred on the Schnee Eifel. Clarke and Hasbrouck would long resent Ridgway for delaying the withdrawal, but the fighting retreat meant that nearly a week went by before the German Fifth Panzer Army controlled St.-Vith and the radiant roads that Manteuffel had hoped to take in two days. "Nobody is worried down here," Ridgway told the First Army by phone at nine P.M. Friday night. "We're in fine shape."

GERMAN TROOPS RANSACKED St.-Vith "in a kind of scavenger hunt," snarling traffic so profoundly that both

Model and Manteuffel dismounted and hiked into town from Schönberg. The field marshal even stood at a crossroads with arms flailing to wave tanks and trucks westward. "Endless columns of prisoners," a Volksgrenadier officer wrote. "Model himself directs traffic."

Looting was best done quickly: beginning on Christmas Day, Allied bombers would drop 1,700 tons of high explosives and incendiaries on St.-Vith, obliterating the train station, reducing most houses to stone dust and ash, and entombing hundreds of Belgian civilians. With roads smashed by the bombs, German engineers routed traffic through the rail yards and along a circuitous dirt track to let the conquerors of St.-Vith continue their pursuit. "We shall throw these arrogant big-mouthed apes from the New World into the sea," a German lieutenant wrote his wife. "They will not get into our Germany."

The bombing of St.-Vith, December 1944.

THE ALLIES' SECRET WEAPON

A GI SHIVERING in an Ardennes foxhole asked, after his first glimpse of a German Me-262 jet streaking overhead, "How come *we* don't ever have any secret weapons?" Yet thousands of enemy troops now sensed what many American soldiers still did not know: that a secret weapon was being used in ground combat for the first time across the bulge, enhancing the killing power of U.S. artillery with what one enthusiast would call "the most remarkable scientific achievement of the war" besides the atomic bomb.

The new weapon's origin dated to 1940 and the recognition that on average 2,500 antiaircraft artillery shells would be needed to bring down a single enemy plane. Both field artillery and antiaircraft rounds exploded either on contact or when a fuse detonated the shell after a preset flight time; neither technique offered killing precision. Scientists and engineers instead sought a fuse that could sense proximity to the target, causing

A German Messerschmitt Swallow

a shell to blow up not when it randomly reached an altitude of ten or fifteen thousand feet, but rather when it detected an airplane within the kill radius of its exploding fragments. Such a fuse would have to be simple enough to build by the millions on an assembly line and sufficiently miniaturized to squeeze into a shell nose roughly the size of an ice-cream cone.

The resulting device, no bigger than a radio tube, was eventually known by the code designation "VT" or "T-98," and by the code name "pozit." It contained a transmitter that broadcast a signal in flight. When the beam bounced off a solid object, a receiver in the fuse detected the reflected signal and tripped a firing circuit that detonated the shell. A five-inch pozit shell, fired by USS *Helena* in the South Pacific, had for the first time brought down a Japanese plane in

January 1943. But for eighteen months, use of the fuse was permitted only over open water or friendly territory, for fear that if the enemy retrieved a dud, their engineers could copy the design.

Pozit variants had been developed for the field artillery, using radio signals bounced off the approaching ground to

Workers prepare armor-piercing shells at a U.S. factory that was converted from aluminum production.

detonate shells fifty or seventy-five feet up. Experiments at army bases in the U.S. showed that regardless of terrain, weather, or darkness, even targets below ground level, such as trenches, were highly vulnerable to a lethal spray of steel shards from such airbursts. One senior army general called it "the most important new development in the ammunition field since the introduction of high explosive projectiles."

With approval from the Joint Chiefs of Staff in late fall, SHAEF fixed Christmas as the day gunners in Europe could open fire with pozit shells. More than a thousand commanders and staff officers were briefed on the secret, with firing demonstrations in six Allied armies. Hitler hastened the debut: when AUTUMN MIST began, Eisenhower moved up the release of the weapon by a week. A gunner in the 99th Infantry Division described "piles of shells with many men using wrenches and hammers to bang off the one [fuse] and install the other." Within days of the first use by field artillerymen, reports described "the slaughter of enemy concentrations east of Bastogne and interdictions of the principal enemy supply routes west of St.-Vith." The 12th Army Group cheerfully reported that the pozit fuse "is a terror weapon." SHAEF concluded that "the enemy has been severely upset."

TRACKING THE MONSTER

THE POZIT WOULD PROVE as demoralizing to German troops as it was heartening to GIs. And no better target could be found for pozit fire than Lieutenant Colonel Peiper's homicidal *Spitze* at the head of the 1st SS Panzer Regiment. For several days, American gunners had been shooting the new shells at the column as it tacked across Belgium.

Peiper's drive toward the Meuse seemed ever more quixotic. When the SS spearhead had turned southwest toward Trois-Ponts, U.S. engineers blew all three bridges there, including one with German soldiers atop the span. Thwarted and desperate for gasoline, Peiper now swung north through broken terrain along the Amblève River, harried by both Allied P-47 fighter-bombers—at least two panzers and five half-tracks were demolished from the air—and artillery. Gunners from the 30th Infantry Division fired three thousand rounds at one bridge approach, cooling their red-hot mortar tubes with cans of water.

Peiper had traveled about sixty miles, but sixteen more still separated him from the Meuse. With the risk of encirclement growing, at dusk on Thursday, December 21, he ordered his men to fall back four miles from Stoumont to La Gleize, a hamlet of thirty houses hemmed in by hills. Here his 1,500 survivors and two dozen remaining tanks dug in with more than a hundred American prisoners in tow.

By late Friday, American machine guns, tanks, tank destroyers, and artillery had so battered La Gleize that SS troops called it *der Kessel* (the Cauldron). Gripping a machine pistol, Peiper dashed between rubble piles, shouting encouragement while his adjutant burned secrets in the cellar. At eight P.M., German transport planes dropped gasoline and ammunition to the besieged men, but GIs recovered most of the supplies except for a few bundles containing cigarettes, schnapps, and a crate of Luger pistols.

"Position considerably worsened. Meager supplies of infantry ammunition left," Peiper radioed early Saturday morning. "This is the last chance of breaking out." Not until two P.M., as the Americans pressed nearer, did permission to retreat arrive in a coded message from I SS Panzer Corps. White-phosphorus and pozit shells carved away the La Gleize church, where German troops sheltered under choir stalls. A soldier caught removing the SS insignia from his uniform was placed against a broken wall and shot for desertion. Peiper used the bombardment to mask the sound of explosives deliberately set to destroy his last twenty-eight panzers, seventy half-tracks, and two dozen guns.

At two A.M. on Sunday, December 24, the SS men crept south from the village in single file, led by two Belgian guides. More than 300 wounded Germans and 130 American prisoners remained behind in the La Gleize cellars. Crossing the Amblève on a small bridge, the column snaked down a ridgeline near Trois-Ponts into the Salm River valley. At daybreak, when spotter planes appeared overhead, Peiper hid his men beneath tree boughs and parceled out provisions: four biscuits and two swigs of cognac each.

Soldiers in the 45th Infantry Division man a machine-gun post near Bastogne. The gun is a Browning M1919 heavy machine gun.

At a ford in the frigid river, the tallest SS troops formed a human chain to help the column cross the forty-foot water gap. Early Christmas morning, Peiper would reach the German line at Wanne, a few miles southeast of La Gleize. Of his original 5,800 men, 770 remained. Hurried along by more gusts of American artillery, their uniforms stiff with ice, they left a bloody track across the snow. Peiper and some of his

A soldier wearing warm winter clothing prepares to cook outside.

henchmen were later accused of murdering 350 unarmed Americans and 100 or more Belgian civilians in their weeklong spree. But for now justice would be deferred, and a day of reckoning delayed until after the war.

All across the Ardennes, heavy snow had been followed on Saturday, December 23, by killing cold in the continental weather phenomenon known as a Russian High. Newspaper correspondent Alan Moorehead described a "radiant world where everything was reduced to primary whites and blues: a strident, sparkling white among the frosted trees, the deep blue shadows in the valley, and then the flawless ice blue of the sky." Radiators and even gas tanks froze. GIs donned every scrap of clothing they could scavenge, including women's dresses worn as shawls.

Troops fashioned sleds from sheet metal, and olive-drab vehicles were daubed with camouflage paint improvised from lime wash and salt. Belgian lace served for helmet nets, and mattress covers, often used as shrouds for the dead, made fine snowsuits. Inflated surgical gloves dipped in paint decorated hospital Christmas trees.

STATUS: GERMANY

CLUMSY SKIRMISHES and pitched battles flared along the front, without deference to the holiday season. Peiper's retreat and the Sixth Panzer Army's shortcomings had extinguished hopes for a German breakthrough; 237,000 American mines, 370 roadblocks, and 70 blown bridges further impeded the north shoulder. In the far south, faltering progress by the Seventh Army had exposed Manteuffel's left flank even as the Fifth Panzer Army tried to capture Bastogne. So desperate were shortages of spare parts and gasoline that new panzers in the Rhine Valley were being cannibalized to avoid burning fuel by sending them intact into battle.

But west of St.-Vith, in the German center, grenadiers vaulted the Salm and Our Rivers, and by December 23, panzer spearheads approached Marche, more than twenty miles beyond Vielsalm and a short bound from Dinant, on the

A photograph captured from the Germans shows soldiers posing on a tank.

Meuse. Model had shoehorned a dozen divisions along a twenty-five-mile battlefront. Although plagued with fuel and ammunition shortages, they remained a potent killing force on the march.

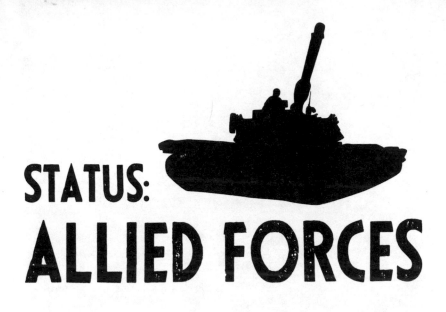

STATUS: ALLIED FORCES

NEW ANXIETY beset First Army headquarters, which had again fallen back, to Tongres, near Maastricht, only hours before German bombs demolished the Hôtel des Bains in Chaudfontaine. Ridgway evinced his usual grit, telling his division commanders by phone at six A.M. on December 24,

> *The situation is normal and entirely satisfactory. The enemy has thrown in all of his mobile reserves, and this is his last major offensive effort in the West in this war. This corps will halt that effort, then attack and smash him.*

The Russian High brought clear skies for the first time since the German attack began, and Allied aircraft took wing in great flocks. In a campaign known as "processing the terrain," twelve thousand offensive sorties were flown in the two days before Christmas, battering highways, airfields, and bridges, as well as rail centers in Koblenz, Trier, and Cologne. Whooping GIs craned their necks as wave upon wave of flying Marauders and Fortresses, Liberators and Lancasters appeared from the west in the heaviest attacks of the war. "The bombers have fine, feathery white streams of vapor streaked across the sky," a 99th Infantry Division soldier wrote his wife, "and the fighters scrawl wavy designs as they try to murder each other." Ice and deep snow entombed German convoys west of the Rhine; horse-drawn plows could hardly clear enough routes for three attacking armies. Model's resupply and reinforcement echelons offered fat targets for Allied fighter-bombers, known as "Jabos" to enemy soldiers. "We prefer to walk instead of using a car on the main highway," a German lieutenant near St.-Vith wrote in his diary. "The American Jabos keep on attacking everything that moves on the roads. . . . [They] hang in the air like a swarm of wasps."

Martin B26 Marauder bombers in formation.

BASTOGNE:
SATURDAY, DECEMBER 23, 1944

CLEAR SKIES also permitted resupply of Bastogne, besieged but unbowed after the rejected surrender ultimatum. Shortly before noon on Saturday, the first C-47s dropped parachute bundles. By four P.M., more than 240 planes had delivered 5,000 artillery shells, almost as many mortar rounds, 2,300 grenades, a dozen boxes of morphine, 300 units of plasma, and 1,500 bandages. Jeeps tore around the drop zone on the western edge of Bastogne, where paratroopers scooped up the bundles and hauled ammunition directly to gun batteries and rifle pits. Flights the next day would bring rations, a quarter million machine-gun rounds, and almost one thousand radio batteries. Brigadier General McAuliffe also had the invaluable services of Captain James E. Parker, a fighter pilot who had arrived several days earlier as an air support officer with enough radio crystals in his pocket to talk directly to the P-47 squadrons now bound for Bastogne. Swarming wasps by the

U.S. troops scan the skies for parachute drops from supply planes, December 1944.

hundreds attacked fast and low with napalm and high explosives, guided by Parker to Manteuffel's panzers, trucks, and assault guns. Tracks in the snow made them easy to find.

Bastogne was reprieved but hardly delivered. German attacks from the west and southwest grew so intense on Saturday night that despondent American officers shook hands good-bye. Despite aerial replenishment, the garrison was reduced to five hundred gallons of gasoline and a day's rations; 101st Airborne Division gunners who had been rationed to ten rounds daily heeded McAuliffe's advice to look for the whites of enemy eyes.

More than three thousand civilians remained trapped with the Americans. Several hundred wounded GIs lay cushioned only by sawdust in a church.

Napalm fires ringed the town, and the chatter of machine guns carried on the wind as the short day faded.

"XMAS PRESENT COMING"

IN THE WHITEWASHED Belgian barracks that served as the 101st headquarters, GIs received a coded message from Patton that afternoon that promised, "Xmas eve present coming up. Hold on." Yet no sign of a relief column from the south had been reported. McAuliffe hid his disappointment from the men but told General Middleton in a phone call, "We have been let down."

At 5:10 P.M., an intrepid pilot in an L-4 Grasshopper, guided by flashlights, landed on a snowy field with a crate of penicillin. That was the last good thing to happen in Bastogne on Christmas Eve. Barely two hours later, beneath a brilliant moon that turned the streets silver, German bombers struck the town in the first of two raids. One bomb landed on an aid station near the Neufchâteau road, caving in the roof, burying twenty soldiers, and killing a civilian nurse. Flames crackled around the Hôtel de Ville. Several patients burned to death on their stretchers on this holiest of holy nights.

PATTON: LUXEMBOURG CITY

DECEMBER 24, 1944

FIFTY MILES AWAY, George Patton was on the move. He had attended a candlelight service on Christmas Eve in the crowded, frigid Episcopal church in Luxembourg City, ensconced with Omar Bradley in a pew once reserved for the German emperor.

Now, scanning the starry sky outside, Patton muttered, "Noel, noel, what a night to give the Nazis hell." Careering about in an open jeep, one pistol holstered outside his parka and another tucked into his waistband, blue eyes watering from the cold, he barked at military police to keep the convoys moving, and he personally challenged sentries to ensure that they knew the day's password.

Patton had made good on his brash promise at Verdun to attack north with three divisions by December 22. It was an enormous feat, requiring most of the Third Army to swing sharply left while keeping the Saar front secure. The maneuver also required distributing fifty-seven tons of new maps, uprooting and reinstalling an extensive signal-wire network, and stockpiling fuel and ammunition, including shells for 1,200 guns in the army's 108 artillery battalions. No SS prisoners were to be taken alive, Patton told his staff. At his urging, an extra skin of armor plate was welded to the front of some Sherman hulls, for a total thickness of four inches. These "Jumbo" tanks were to lead the columns churning north. "Drive like hell," Patton urged. "We have an opportunity of winning the war."

There were many missteps. Poor radio security allowed German eavesdroppers to track Third Army troop movements, tank crews failed to sweep the snow off their fluorescent recognition panels and were strafed by their own P-47s, and many skidding wrecks were caused by the hard freeze. When the 4th Armored Division was seven miles south of Bastogne, Patton ordered a perilous night attack that gained only four hundred yards and left one tank battalion with just fourteen Shermans instead of the usual fifty. A German ambush in Chaumont smacked a combat command back more than a mile at a cost of eleven more Shermans and thirty-six hours. "The troops built little fires of anything that would burn," an armored officer wrote. "The dead lay frozen and stiff and when the men came to load them in trucks, they picked them up and put them in like big logs of wood."

"This was probably my fault, because I had been insisting on day and night attacks," Patton confessed in his diary. Even

Tankmen of the First Army gather around a fire to open Christmas packages, December 30, 1944.

after almost four decades as a soldier, he reflected on how "it takes a long time to learn war . . . to really learn how to fight." He had predicted that the Third Army would reach Bastogne on December 24, but with the 4th Armored Division making little progress—German paratroopers kept reinfiltrating cleared villages—Patton twice phoned an irate Eisenhower to apologize for delays. "This snow is God-awful," he said. "I'm sorry."

Early Christmas morning, in search of a seam through enemy defenses, Combat Command R looped thirty miles from the 4th Armored Division's right flank to the division's far left, near Neufchâteau. The 37th Tank Battalion led the attack north under Lieutenant Colonel Creighton W. Abrams, Jr. When a blown bridge halted the battalion, Abrams, chewing a cigar, ordered a bulldozer to demolish a stone wall and push the debris into the creek to create a causeway.

On Monday afternoon, December 26, the battalion crested a ridge three miles southwest of the Bastogne perimeter. Thirteen artillery batteries fired more than five hundred rounds into the farm village of Assenois. With friendly shells falling close enough to wound several GIs, Shermans and half-tracks charged through streets darkened by smoke and dust, as Volksgrenadiers poured from the cellars in what the official history would call a "shooting, clubbing, stabbing mêlée." Before surrendering with five hundred other defenders, a German officer reported by telephone, "They are through Assenois and going to Bastogne."

Five Shermans and a half-track raced north under Lieutenant Charles Boggess. Gunfire ripped through the fir trees, shooting down surprised Germans standing in a mess line, and three tank shells killed a dozen more in a concrete blockhouse. Boggess spotted colored parachutes scattered in a field and foxholes flanking the road ahead. "Come here!" he yelled, standing in his turret. "This is the 4th Armored." Several helmeted figures in olive drab emerged from their holes, and at 4:50 P.M., the siege of Bastogne was over. Twenty minutes later, McAuliffe greeted Abrams politely: "It's good to see you, Colonel."

"Kilroy Was Stuck Here," someone had chalked on the charred wall of a ruined barn. Now that graffiti liberator had himself been liberated. Seventy ambulances and supply trucks soon rolled into the smoldering town, and seven hundred enemy prisoners marched out; a 101st Airborne Division sergeant scrutinized their footwear, smashing his

rifle butt onto the toes of any German wearing GI boots. The eight-day defense of a drab market town in Belgium had cost more than two thousand American casualties. Losses in the 4th Armored Division added an additional thousand to the tally, and the division's tank strength hardly equaled that

In late December 1944, American troops walk through the ruined streets of Bastogne, Belgium.

Generals Anthony McAuliffe (left) and George Patton (right) confer in Bastogne.

of a battalion. But Rundstedt's chief of staff would later list the "failure to conquer Bastogne" first among seven factors that caused AUTUMN MIST to fail.

Patton had his own assessment. Never averse to historical grandiosity, he told reporters a few days later that the battle at Bastogne would be considered "just as important as the battle of Gettysburg was to the Civil War."

"GLORY HAS ITS PRICE"

General Dwight D. Eisenhower

IN THE LAST WEEK of December, *Time* magazine chose Eisenhower as its "Man of the Year." A flattering cover portrait depicted the supreme commander flanked by American and British flags, with legions of soldiers and tanks stretching behind him into the middle distance. The honor rang a bit tinny, given the current German salient in Allied territory, which now measured forty miles wide by sixty miles deep. U.S. losses in the last two weeks of December included almost 600 tanks, 1,400 jeeps, 700 trucks, 2,400 machine guns, 1,700 bazookas, 5,000 rifles, and 65,000 overcoats. The enemy had accumulated such a large number of American vehicles that pilots were ordered to bomb any column that included both Allied and German models.

Of greater concern was a German armored spearhead ripping a seam between U.S. VIII Corps in the south and XVIII Airborne Corps in the north. Fatigue, dispersion, empty fuel tanks, and ammunition shortages impaired the enemy drive. In some instances, half a German brigade towed the other half, and supply trucks often had to make a four-night round-trip drive to Bonn for artillery shells. Despite it all, on Christmas Day the 2nd Panzer Division was only five miles from Dinant, soon drawing near enough to the Meuse River crossings to draw fire from British tanks.

For the past week, Eisenhower had been looking for counteroffensive opportunities that would trap the over-extended Germans and fulfill his ambition of annihilating enemy forces west of the Rhine River. An Ultra intercept decoded just after Christmas revealed that Model's army group was fast running short of serviceable tanks and assault guns; despite recent losses, the U.S. First, Third, and Ninth Armies alone had almost four thousand tanks.

But disagreement over when and where to strike back divided Allied commanders.

Patton favored driving from the south through the base of the German salient, toward Bitburg and then east, in hopes of bagging the entire enemy pocket. Major General J. Lawton Collins, commander of VII Corps, in a memorandum on Wednesday,

Field Marshal Walter Model (center), one of two senior commanders of the German army in the west.

December 27, laid out three options and endorsed "Plan No. 2," a strong attack from the north toward St.-Vith, complemented by the Third Army's lunge from the south. Montgomery hesitated, suspecting that Rundstedt had enough combat strength for another attack that could punch through the Americans to Liège. Collins thought not. "Nobody is going to break through these troops," he told Montgomery. "This isn't going to happen." If the Allies failed to attack closer to the base of the salient, they risked leaving a corridor through which retreating Germans could escape, he told the field marshal. "You're going to push the Germans out of the bag," Collins added.

But now Montgomery turned cautious, perhaps discouraged by the First Army's early defeats. He had doubted Patton's ability to reach Bastogne or impede Manteuffel, and he

Supreme Commander Eisenhower (center left) confers with Generals Bradley and Patton (right). With them is Sergeant Jules Grad, an American military reporter (far left).

doubted that the poor roads leading south toward St.-Vith would support Collins's scheme. Rather than gamble on an attempt by the First and Third Armies to sever the forty-mile base of the salient, he thought a more prudent counterstrike would aim the two armies' main blows across the waist of the bulge at Houffalize, north of Bastogne, shooing away the enemy rather than trapping him, and only after the German offensive had, as he put it, "definitely expended itself."

Eisenhower chafed at Montgomery's caution. Patton wrote in his diary the same day, "War requires the taking of risks and he won't take them." Yet others were just as circumspect as Montgomery. Beetle Smith, in a staff meeting on Wednesday, suggested telling "our masters in Washington that if they want us to win the war over here they must find us another ten divisions." Bradley also favored pinching the enemy at Houffalize, not least because Eisenhower had promised to return the First Army to his command when the town fell. First Army planners agreed that poor roads precluded hitting the base of the Ardennes salient, and Colonel Benjamin "Monk" Dickson, the intelligence chief, endorsed Montgomery's view that Rundstedt could strike again; he counted seventeen uncommitted German divisions. Deteriorating weather further encouraged prudence: a five-day spell of clear skies ended on Thursday, December 28, and with it the comfort provided by Allied air fleets.

INSURRECTION IN THE NORTH

DELAYED BY FOG, snowbanks, and further reports of assassins afoot, Eisenhower's command train pulled into a rail siding in the Belgian town of Hasselt, five miles south of Zonhoven, early Thursday afternoon, December 28. Bodyguards bounded through the station, searching for potential assassins, and machine-gun crews crouched on the platform to lay down a suppressive cross fire if needed. Montgomery hopped aboard at 2:30 P.M. to find Eisenhower in his study, eager to discuss a counteroffensive that would turn the tables in the Ardennes once and for all. While Beetle Smith and Francis "Freddie" de Guingand, the two chiefs of staff, waited in an unheated corridor, Montgomery sketched the plan: four corps would squeeze the enemy salient from the north and northwest, complementing the three already attacking from the south under Patton. The two wings would plan to meet in Houffalize, halfway down the length of the bulge.

Field Marshal Montgomery (center) was put in temporary command of the armies of (left to right) British Lieutenant General Dempsey, U.S. Lieutenant General Hodges, U.S. Lieutenant General Simpson, and Canadian General Crerar.

Yet the field marshal was vague about precisely when this cataclysmic counterblow would fall. Building a combat reserve was vital, Montgomery said. His own direct observation and the intelligence gathered by his "gallopers"—young British liaison officers who reported to him personally from far corners of the battlefield—led him to conclude that the First Army still lacked the strength to confront an enemy force that included at least seven panzer divisions with enough residual power to launch "at least one more full-blooded attack." Better to let the enemy first impale himself with a final, futile lunge toward the Meuse. Then, deflecting Eisenhower's impatient request for a firm date, Montgomery urged development of a "master plan for the future conduct of war," one in which "all available offensive power must be allotted to the northern front," preferably with a single commander who "must have powers of operational control."

With this ancient theme again resurrected, Eisenhower brought the meeting to a close and showed Montgomery to the platform. Machine-gunners folded their tripods, bodyguards reboarded, and the train returned to Versailles by way of Brussels. Despite Montgomery's insistence that the necessary conditions fall into place before an Allied counterblow was launched, the supreme commander believed that he had extracted a commitment for an attack from the north to begin in four days, on Monday, January 1.

That was incorrect. Montgomery returned to his field camp in Zonhoven and cabled Alan Brooke that Eisenhower was "definitely in a somewhat humble frame of mind and clearly realizes that the present trouble would not have occurred if he had accepted British advice and not that of American generals." He further believed, after a recent conference with Bradley, that the latter had also finally recognized the limitations of his generalship. "Poor chap," Montgomery had written Brooke, "he is such a decent fellow and the whole thing is a bitter pill for him." But the 21st Army Group had put the Allies back on track. "We have tidied up the mess," he told the British chief, "and got two American armies properly organized." Montgomery also wanted the War Office to know that although he cabled London about his operations each night, no such report went to SHAEF. "You are far better informed, and in the picture, than is Ike," he confided.

And then he overplayed his hand. In a note to Eisenhower on Friday, December 29, Montgomery wrote,

We have had one very definite failure. . . . One commander must have powers to direct and control the operation; you cannot possibly do it yourself, and so you would have to nominate someone else.

He enclosed a proposed order for Eisenhower to issue to both 12th and 21st Army Groups, decreeing that "from now onwards full operational direction, control, and coordination of these operations is vested in the [commander in chief of] 21 Army Group." In summation, he told the supreme commander, "I put this matter up to you again only because I am so anxious not to have another failure." However, he added, without "one man directing and controlling . . . we will fail again."

By chance, Montgomery's note arrived just before a personal message to Eisenhower from Chief of Staff George Marshall, who noted that "certain London papers" were calling for the field marshal to command "all your ground forces." The chief added,

Under no circumstances make any concessions of any kind whatsoever. You not only have our complete confidence but there would be a terrific resentment in this country following such action. . . . Give them hell.

The supreme commander's patience finally snapped when the agreeable Major General de Guingand arrived in Versailles on Saturday, December 30, with the disagreeable news that no offensive would be launched from the north until at least January 3, leaving Patton to fight alone in the south against a ferociously reinforced enemy. Convinced that he had been deceived, Eisenhower stormed about his office, ordering staff officers to find the message confirming Montgomery's commitment to a January 1 attack—a futile search, de Guingand assured him, because "knowing Monty, the last thing he would do is commit himself on paper."

"All right, Beetle," Eisenhower said, turning to his chief of staff. "I'm going to send a telegram . . . to the Joint Chiefs of Staff that I've had trouble with this man and it's either they can relieve me if they'd like to—that would be perfectly all right—but one of the two of us has to go."

Now fully aware of Montgomery's peril, and of Marshall's stern note and the thinly concealed American yen to have British Field Marshal Sir Harold Alexander command the 21st Army Group, de Guingand proposed driving immediately to Zonhoven. "Won't you please hold up that telegram till I get back?" he asked Eisenhower.

"All right, Freddie, I'll hold this up until tomorrow morning. But I don't think you ought to try and get up there, not tonight, because the weather is so bad."

After de Guingand hurried out to begin the treacherous two-hundred-mile drive to Montgomery's headquarters, Eisenhower dictated a frosty cable to the field marshal:

I do not agree that one army group commander should fight his own battle and give orders to another army group commander. . . . You disturb me by predictions of "failure" unless your exact opinions in the matter of giving you command over Bradley are met in detail. I assure you that in this matter I can go no further. . . . We would have to present our differences to the CC/S [Combined Chiefs of Staff].

Already in fragile health, de Guingand arrived in Zonhoven at midnight, as Alan Moorehead later told Forrest Pogue, "nearly exhausted, a little hysterical, full of whisky. . . . He said to Monty, 'I must see you at once.'" As the chief of staff described the surly mood in Versailles, Montgomery paced around his caravan.

"If you keep on, one of you will have to go," de Guingand said, "and it won't be Ike."

A German tank passes American prisoners of war,
December 17, 1944.

Montgomery scoffed. "Who would replace me?"

"That's already been worked out," de Guingand said. "They want Alex."

Montgomery's bluster abruptly dissolved. "What shall I do, Freddie?" he asked. "What shall I do?"

De Guingand had already drafted an apology to Eisenhower, which he now pulled from his battle dress. "Sign this," he said. Montgomery scratched his signature and arranged to have the message delivered, marked "eyes only":

Dear Ike . . . Whatever your decision may be you can rely on me one hundred percent to make it work and I know Brad will do the same. Very distressed that my letter may have upset you and I would ask you to tear it up. Your very devoted subordinate, Monty.

The crisis passed, but the scars would linger. Soon after sending his apologetic note to Eisenhower, Montgomery privately cabled Brooke, "The general tendency at SHAEF and among the American command is one of considerable optimism. . . . I cannot share this optimism." Eisenhower thanked Montgomery for "your very fine telegram," but the incessant friction with the field marshal kept him awake at night. "He's just a little man," he would say after the war. "He's just as little inside as he is outside."

INSURRECTION
IN THE SOUTH

NO SOONER had Eisenhower suppressed this insurrection on his northern flank than his southern flank erupted, first with insubordination by the 6th Army Group, then in a German attack.

The first started with Lieutenant General Jacob Devers, commander of ten French and eight American divisions. Devers had accomplished little in Alsace because Eisenhower refused to let him move forward and cross the Rhine River near Strasbourg. Since then, his troops had been scattered by orders to attack in opposite directions: north, to shore up Bradley's flank, and south, to help eradicate a small enemy salient around Colmar. Neither had yielded conspicuous success.

At Verdun on December 19, Eisenhower had ordered Devers's 6th Army Group to help Bradley in the bulge by contributing troops and shifting to the defensive. Three days later, Devers halted further attacks against the Colmar Pocket, leaving Hitler still master of 850 square miles of France. But Eisenhower was willing to cede much more: a SHAEF staff officer on December 26 brought Devers a map drawn by the supreme commander personally, which made plain that the Franco-American armies were to fall back nearly forty miles to an ostensibly more defensible line along the Vosges Mountains, abandoning Strasbourg and the Alsatian plain. Devers flew to Versailles on December 27 to argue that a retreat from the Rhine would anger the French and embolden the Germans. Eisenhower stood fast, spooked by intelligence reports of German legions massing across from the U.S. Seventh Army. The 6th Army Group, he told Devers, must move "back to the Vosges line and hang on" until the Ardennes struggle subsided. Supply dumps were to be shifted into the mountains, and Devers was to keep two U.S. divisions, one armored and one infantry, as a reserve west of the Vosges. Devers wrote in his diary,

The Germans undoubtedly will attack me now. . . . The position I give up is much stronger than the one to which I go. . . . Giving up the town of Strasbourg is a political disaster to France.

General Charles de Gaulle, leader of the Free French Forces, thought so too. His troops were passionately patriotic. On December 28, de Gaulle sent General Alphonse Juin, the

French military chief of staff, to Versailles to make inquiries about a rumored retreat in Alsace. Juin cornered Beetle Smith, who told him that no firm decision had been made and that SHAEF's action was "simply the study of a plan." In truth, Smith had drafted the final order that morning. Juin motored back and warned de Gaulle, "They are up to something."

Meanwhile, Lieutenant General Devers decided to obey part of his order. He moved his command post seventy miles west, to Vittel, but ordered his staff to prepare plans for three intermediate fallback positions leading to a final line along the eastern face of the Vosges. When General Alexander "Sandy" Patch was told to ready his Seventh Army for withdrawal, he winked at a staff officer and said, "Ain't going to do it. We aren't that bad off."

The French general Jean de Lattre de Tassigny was even more stubborn, wondering why he should retreat and then have to recapture the same ground again. He took two days to translate Devers's withdrawal directive into his own "General Order No. 201," which on December 30 instructed French subordinates "to maintain the integrity of the present front" by yielding not a single square centimeter of Alsatian soil. Devers cabled

Lieutenant General Jacob Devers, commander of the U.S. 6th Army Group

*Generals Charles de Gaulle (center left) and
Alphonse Juin (right) early in the war.*

Eisenhower that falling back to the Vosges could take two weeks.

The supreme commander's neck flushed deep red. "Call up Devers and tell him he is not doing what he was told," he barked at Smith. "Tell him to obey his orders and shorten his line." Getting the phone call in Vittel, Devers feebly claimed that Eisenhower's earlier instruction had been discretionary. "I won't go to him with that story," Smith snapped. "He thinks you've been disloyal." Another written order from Eisenhower left no wiggle room:

> *The political pressure to retain French soil, which you*
> *are undoubtedly experiencing, must be resisted if it*

leads to any risk of your losing divisions. . . . You must not endanger the integrity of your units east of your main position, the Vosges. You must be prepared to accept the loss of territory east of the Vosges and all its political consequences.

Devers gave in, telling subordinates that all forces would have to retreat to the Vosges no later than January 5. "Eisenhower," he wrote in his diary, "has given me no alternative." As for the supreme commander, Eisenhower was now so vexed at a man whom he had long disliked that he considered firing Devers and giving command of his army group to Seventh Army General Patch.

"You can kill a willing horse by overdoing what you require of him," Devers wrote in his diary. "SHAEF has given me too much front, and taken away too many of my troops. This is unsound."

THE **LAST** GERMAN GROUND OFFENSIVE

JANUARY 1, 1945

THE FINAL DAY of the year had ticked by with fresh snow and more omens. A reconnaissance flight at last light detected German artillery lumbering forward into new gun pits. The U.S. Seventh Army placed all its troops on high alert and canceled holiday celebrations. A reporter who insisted on toasting the departure of 1944 declared, "Never was the world plagued by such a year less worth remembering." Devers's diary entry for December 31 was just as cheerless: "Patch called me. . . . He was sure he was going to be attacked during the night."

The land attack indeed fell that night, the last substantial German offensive of the war in western Europe. Hitler had given another pep talk to commanders in Army Group G, conceding failure in the Ardennes but offering another chance to thrash the Americans in Operation NORDWIND (NORTH WIND).

A German soldier fires a flare.

A lunge by eight divisions southwest down the Vosges would recapture the Saverne Gap and link up with Nineteenth Army troops still holding out in the Colmar Pocket; in addition, the attack would force Patton to withdraw from Bastogne to deal with this new threat. French troops in Alsace were weak and disorganized, the Führer promised, and the U.S. Seventh Army was overextended along a 126-mile perimeter.

The Americans were also alert and entrenched. Ultra intercepts provided no specific enemy attack order, but ample intelligence revealed that the main offensive would come against the Seventh Army left, west of the Haardt Mountains, with a complementary attack to the east between the mountains and the Rhine.

"German offensive began on Seventh Army front about 0030 hours," Patch's chief of staff wrote in a diary entry on Monday, January 1. "Krauts were howling drunk. Murdered them." Shrieking SS troops, silhouetted by moonlight that glistened off snowfields near the Sarre River, hardly dented the American left wing. A single .30-caliber water-cooled machine gun, spewing left and right with long, chattering bursts, was credited with slaying more than one hundred

German soldiers run for cover.

attackers. "Gained only insignificant ground," the German Army Group G war diary recorded; then, by nightfall on Tuesday: "The attack has lost its momentum."

The most flamboyant German sally occurred on New Year's Day, an air attack by nine hundred German planes flying at treetop altitude across the Western Front. Operation BODEN-PLATTE (BASEPLATE) included pilots said to be wearing dress uniforms with patent-leather shoes and white gloves after celebrating the arrival of 1945. The raiders caught seventeen Allied airfields by surprise, destroying 150 parked planes and damaging more than 100 others. Montgomery's personal aircraft was among those wrecked. But German losses approached 300 planes, some shot down by their own antiaircraft gunners who, for reasons of secrecy, had not been informed of BASEPLATE. Worse still was the loss of 237 German pilots, including veteran airmen, instructors, and commanders. "We sacrificed our last substance," one Luftwaffe officer said.

Even as NORTH WIND collapsed on the German right, a secondary New Year's attack ten miles to the east by the German 6th SS Mountain Division bent the U.S. Seventh Army line sufficiently to alarm SHAEF and

A German pilot suited up and ready.

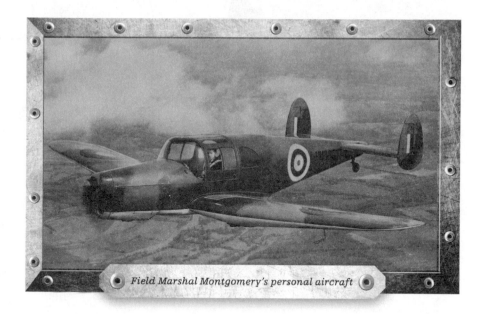

Field Marshal Montgomery's personal aircraft

terrify the citizens of Strasbourg, thirty miles southeast. German propaganda broadcasts from Radio Stuttgart reported shock troops assembling to seize the city, with reprisals certain to fall on citizens who had helped the Allies. Rumors of U.S. Seventh Army detachments packing to leave along the Rhine "spread like a powder fuse and caused a general panic," according to a French lieutenant.

Lowered French flags and the sight of official sedans being gassed up added to the dread. Journalists reported that roads west were clogged with "women pushing baby carriages [and] wagons piled high with furniture" as Strasbourg steeled itself for yet another reversal of fortune. One soldier spied inverted dinner plates laid across a road in the thin hope that they sufficiently resembled antitank mines to delay, at least briefly, the Germans' return.

THE **INTERNAL FIGHT** FOR
STRASBOURG

CHARLES DE GAULLE, referring to himself in the third person, declared that the abandonment of Strasbourg would not only be "a terrible wound inflicted on the honor of the country," but also "a profound blow to the nation's confidence in de Gaulle." On Tuesday, January 2, he told de Lattre in a handwritten note, "Naturally the French Army cannot consent to the abandonment of Strasbourg.... I order you to take matters into your own hands." At nearly the same moment, Devers cabled de Lattre to pull his left wing back toward the Vosges no later than Friday morning, necessarily exposing the city. The American order had "a bomb-like effect" in the French army headquarters, one staff officer observed, and it provoked an anguished *"Ça, non!"* from de Lattre, now confronted by conflicting orders from two masters in what he called "a grave problem of conscience."

De Gaulle saw no dilemma. When de Lattre proposed waiting "until the Allied high command has given its consent" to defend Strasbourg, de Gaulle replied, "I cannot accept your last communication." De Lattre's sole duty, de Gaulle added, was to France. Strasbourg's mayor sent the army commander a photograph of the city's spectacular cathedral with an inscription, *To General de Lattre, our last hope.*

At nine P.M. on Tuesday, General Juin appeared at Beetle Smith's office in Versailles and spent five hours warning of "extremely grave consequences" that would cause "the supreme commander to be severely judged" should Strasbourg be abandoned. After repeating himself incessantly, at two A.M. Juin pulled from his pocket a letter in which de Gaulle threatened to withdraw French forces from SHAEF command. "We are dependent on them," de Gaulle had told Juin, "but inversely they are dependent on us."

"Juin said things to me last night, which, if he had been an American, I would have socked him on the jaw," a bleary-eyed Smith told Eisenhower during a staff meeting Wednesday morning, January 3. For more than an hour in the supreme commander's office, joined by the intelligence chief, Kenneth Strong, and the commander of the Strategic Air Forces in Europe, Carl Spaatz, they debated their course. Smith still believed that withdrawal to the Vosges was imperative; the 6th Army Group reported pressure across the entire front from NORTH WIND. Devers had now accepted Eisenhower's order "to forget Strasbourg," but to forsake the city would threaten Allied unity. Strasbourg's military governor had warned

The streets of Strasbourg, France, when it was liberated in November 1944.

General Patch, "You will cover the American flag with ineradicable shame," and dispatches from the city at five that morning predicted "terrible reprisals" and "mass massacres." Evacuation plans had already been drafted to begin with a thousand civil servants that afternoon, although only two hundred railcars were available to transport at least a hundred thousand civilians. Buffeted by contradictory demands, de Lattre appeared to have fallen in step with de Gaulle by ordering the 3rd Algerian Division to prepare for deployment to Strasbourg.

"Next to the weather," Eisenhower would tell George Marshall, the French "have caused me more trouble in this war than any other single factor. They even rank above landing craft." The art of command at times requires tactical retreat for strategic advantage, in a headquarters no less than on a battlefield. By midday on Wednesday, the supreme commander sensibly recognized that in the interest of Allied harmony, he would have to yield. De Gaulle had requested a meeting at three P.M., but before formally acceding to French demands, Eisenhower intended to land a punch or two.

Smith phoned Devers to ask how close German forces were to the Alsatian capital.

"About thirty miles," Devers replied.

"Well, keep them as far away as you can," Smith said. "It looks now as if you will have to hold Strasbourg."

Strasbourg is a city famous for its bridges and magnificent cathedral.

WINSTON CHURCHILL ARRIVES

General Dwight Eisenhower and Prime Minister Winston Churchill, date unknown

THE CROWDED STAGE in this melodrama grew more congested at 2:15 P.M. with the arrival of Prime Minister Winston Churchill and Field Marshal Alan Brooke after a turbulent flight from England. Eisenhower whisked them from the airfield to his house for a quick lunch, and then to a conference room in the Trianon Palace. De Gaulle soon appeared, stiff and unsmiling, with Juin on his heels. The men settled into armchairs arranged in a circle around a situation map spread across the floor, and de Gaulle handed Eisenhower a copy of his letter ordering de Lattre to defend Strasbourg.

Eisenhower gestured to the map of Alsace, which showed three German corps bearing down from the north, as well as half a dozen enemy divisions threatening attack from the Colmar salient. "In Alsace, where the enemy has extended his attack for two days, the Colmar Pocket makes our position a precarious one," he said. The long front exposed French and American soldiers alike. Moreover, Devers not only had no reserves, he had been told to forfeit two divisions to reinforce the Ardennes, where fighting remained savage.

Prime Minister Churchill and General de Gaulle, January 1944

"Alsace is sacred ground," de Gaulle replied. Allowing the Germans to regain Strasbourg could bring down the French government, leading to "a state bordering on anarchy in the entire country."

"All my life," Churchill said pleasantly, "I have remarked what significance Alsace has for the French."

Even so, Eisenhower said, he resented being pressured to amend military plans for political reasons. The threat to pull French forces from SHAEF command seemed spiteful, given all that the Allies had done for France; the Combined Chiefs already had agreed to equip sixteen French divisions, and de Gaulle had recently asked for a total of fifty. Should *le général* choose to fight independently, SHAEF would have no choice but to suspend supplies of fuel and munitions to the French army. This crisis could have been averted, Eisenhower added, had de Lattre's troops fought well and eradicated the Colmar Pocket, as ordered.

By now the supreme commander's face had grown beet red. De Gaulle stared down his great nose. General Eisenhower, he said, was at "risk of seeing the outraged French people forbid the use of its railroads and communications. . . . If you carry out the withdrawal, I will give the order to a French division to barricade itself inside Strasbourg and before the scandalized world you will be obliged to go in and free it."

Having lost his composure, Eisenhower now regained it. Very well, he conceded, Strasbourg would be defended. Sacred Alsace would remain French, the withdrawal order to Devers canceled.

The conference ended. "I think you've done the wise and proper thing," Churchill told Eisenhower. Buttonholing de Gaulle in a corridor outside, the prime minister said, in his fractured French, that Eisenhower was "not always aware of the political consequences of his decisions" but was nonetheless "an excellent supreme commander." De Gaulle said nothing, but before Eisenhower bade him adieu at the front door of the Trianon Palace, de Gaulle told him, "Glory has its price. Now you are going to be a conqueror."

As the happy news of salvation spread through Strasbourg late Wednesday afternoon, jubilant crowds belted out "La Marseillaise." The French tricolor flag rose again before the police barracks, and a Seventh Army loudspeaker truck rolled through the city, urging calm. Eisenhower authorized Devers to keep the new SHAEF reserve for his own use; Strasbourg was to be defended "as strongly as possible"—primarily by French troops—but without risking "the integrity of your forces, which will not be jeopardized."

NORTH WIND would drag on, with three more attacks against the Americans by large numbers of German troops, and another against the French up the Rhine–Rhône Canal from Colmar. The Seventh Army's right wing bent back ten miles and more, particularly along the Rhine near Haguenau, and enemy troops ferried across the river at Gambsheim got to within a few miles of Strasbourg before being cuffed back. But these

Troops on a bridge over the Rhine River.

small territorial gains, which cost twenty-three thousand irreplaceable German casualties, carried little strategic heft; Patch held the Saverne Gap and the Rhine–Marne Canal, and Patton was not diverted from the Ardennes. Hitler denounced as "pessimistic" reports from Alsace that NORTH WIND had failed for want of sufficient infantry. Yet he was reduced to using Volksgrenadiers who had trained together for only a month, among them recruits from eastern Europe who spoke no German and a convalescent unit known as the "Whipped Cream Division" because of its special dietary needs.

"We must believe in the ultimate purposes of a merciful God," Eisenhower had written Mamie after his confrontation with de Gaulle. "These are trying days." Rarely had the burden of command weighed more heavily on him. Bodyguards still shadowed his every move, he found no time for exercise, and despite his regular letters home, his wife chided him for not writing often enough.

NEW WORRIES

EISENHOWER HAD NEW worries too. Recent intelligence suggested the Germans might soon use poison gas on the battlefield. It was also said that enemy scientists were developing a ray capable of stopping Allied aircraft engines in flight.

Further, Eisenhower suffered yet another significant loss: on January 2, ice on the wings combined with pilot error during takeoff had caused a twin-engine Hudson to crash at airfield A-46, five miles south of Versailles. The fiery accident killed British Admiral Bertram Ramsay—among Eisenhower's staunchest and most valued advisers—who was flying to Brussels for a conference with Montgomery about the defenses at Antwerp. On Sunday, January 7, a French naval band played Chopin's funeral march as a gun carriage bore Ramsay's coffin to a hillside grave above the Seine. The supreme commander joined mourners in the shuffling procession.

Later that afternoon, Eisenhower's office calendar recorded, "E. leaves office early, 4:30 & goes home. He is very depressed these days."

Admiral Sir Bertram Ramsay in London, 1944

YARD
BY YARD

U.S. troops wear white bedsheets as camouflage on their march near Faymonville, Belgium, January 16, 1945.

A FINAL GERMAN lunge at Bastogne lingered, with fighting as fierce as any seen in the Ardennes. The number of German divisions battling the Third Army increased from three to nine. Dreadful weather again grounded much of the Allied air force and forced American gunners to use blowtorches and pinch bars to free frozen gun carriages. Patton had hoped to seize Houffalize in a one-day bound of seventeen miles; instead, his drive north with III and VIII Corps averaged barely a mile a day, arriving on January 9. First Army's attack from the north, finally launched by Montgomery on January 3, moved no faster. Fog, snow, mines, rugged terrain, blown bridges, and a stubborn enemy reduced Collins's VII Corps to a crawl and cost five thousand casualties in the plodding advance on Houffalize.

On January 8, Hitler authorized Model to at last abandon

the western half of the bulge, but not for three days did GIs see signs of a general withdrawal, yard by grudging yard. On January 14, the Führer rejected a plea from Rundstedt and Model to pull back to the Rhine; the retreat instead must halt at the Siegfried Line, where the offensive had begun almost four years previously.

At 11:40 A.M. on Tuesday, January 16, an Allied cavalry patrol from the north met an Allied armored infantry patrol from the south outside Houffalize to link the First and Third Armies. This was the beginning of the end of this hard contest. The bulge, harboring the enemy for a month, had been punctured.

A day later, Eisenhower returned the U.S. First Army to Omar Bradley's command. First Army commander Courtney

The wreckage of a German tank destroyed near Bastogne.

German prisoners under guard.

Hodges sent Montgomery five pounds of coffee as thanks for his ministrations, and on January 18 moved the army headquarters back to the Hôtel Britannique in Spa. The place was largely intact, except that the furniture had been upended and a Christmas tree, with its ornaments missing, was "tilting drunkenly in one corner." The Ninth Army would remain for a time under British command, despite complaints from Bradley, who finally took SHAEF's hint by shifting his command post from isolated Luxembourg City to Namur, the city in Belgium where the Meuse and Sambre Rivers meet.

Village by village, farm by farm, American soldiers

reclaimed what they had lost. Major General Troy Middleton deployed his VIII Corps headquarters back to Bastogne, where 101st Airborne Division paratroopers gave him a receipt certifying that the town was "used but serviceable" and "Kraut disinfected." The 7th Armored Division reentered ruined

A soldier in his bivouac guards the road, bazooka at the ready.

St.-Vith on January 23, capturing a German artillery officer whose latest diary entry read, "The battle noises come closer to the town. . . . I'm sending back all my personal belongings. One never knows."

Soldiers watch for snipers at St.-Vith, January 23, 1945.

"I KNOW THE WAR IS LOST"

HITLER LEFT the Adlerhorst at six P.M. on January 15 and returned to Berlin the next morning aboard the *Brandenburg*. There would be no jackboots in Antwerp or even across the Meuse, no dividing of Allied armies, no petitions for peace from Washington and London. "I know the war is lost," he said, according to a staff officer. "The superior power is too great. I've been betrayed." Still, Hitler had extracted his armies from the Ardennes at a deliberate pace and in good order. Manteuffel abandoned fifty-three tanks along the roadside on a single day for want of fuel or spare parts, but many other tanks returned to Germany. In the south alone, thirteen divisions from the Fifth Panzer Army and the Seventh Army crossed five bridges thrown over the Our. The enemy, Eisenhower admitted, "will probably manage to withdraw the bulk of his formations." Nearly two weeks would pass after the capture of Houffalize before the

Adolf Hitler, January 30, 1942

retreating Germans slammed the last steel door in the West Wall.

In the west, the war receded for good. Once again Belgium and Luxembourg had been liberated. Children shrieked with joy while sledding near a stone quarry in Luxembourg, oblivious to the heckle of Thunderbolt cannons above the retreating enemy just to the east. The milky contrails of bombers bound for Cologne or Duisburg or Berlin etched the sky from horizon to horizon. Across the Ardennes, women stood in their doorways, eyeing the olive-drab ranks tramping by. "Are you sure?" they asked. "Are you sure they have really gone for good?"

The liberation of Colmar, France, on February 2, 1945.

The dead "lay thick," wrote American war correspondent Martha Gellhorn as the guns fell silent, "like some dark shapeless vegetable." For weeks, the frozen ground was as hard as iron and precluded burials, except with earthmoving equipment and jackhammers; many of the three thousand civilians killed in the Ardennes were wrapped in blankets and stored in church crypts to await a thaw. At the Henri-Chapelle American Cemetery in Hombourg, Belgium, grave diggers with backhoes worked around the clock to bury as many as five hundred GIs a day. Each was interred in a hole five feet deep, two feet wide, and six and a half feet long, but only after his overshoes had been removed for reuse. One dog tag was placed in the dead man's mouth; the other was tacked to a cross or a Star of David atop the grave. Those whose tags had been lost went to a morgue tent for photographs and dental charting. Fingertips were cleaned and injected with fluid to enhance prints, while technicians searched for laundry marks, tattoos, and other identifying clues, all to avoid conceding that here was yet another mother's son known only to God.

Among the dead gathered by Graves Registration teams combing the bulge were those murdered by Peiper's men near Malmédy, recovered in two feet of snow when the Baugnez crossroad was recaptured in mid-January. Investigators carried the frozen corpses, stiff as statuary, to a heated shed. There, field jackets and trouser pockets were

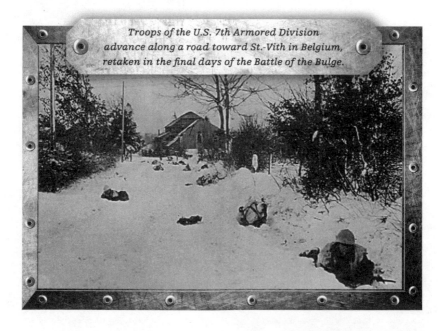

Troops of the U.S. 7th Armored Division advance along a road toward St.-Vith in Belgium, retaken in the final days of the Battle of the Bulge.

sliced open with razor blades to inventory the effects, like those of Technician Fifth Grade Luke S. Swartz—"one fountain pen, two pencils, one New Testament, one comb, one good-luck charm"—and Private First Class Robert Cohen, who left this world carrying thirteen coins, two cigarette lighters, and a prayer book in Hebrew.

AN ARMY TALLY long after the war put combined U.S. battle losses in the Ardennes and Alsace from December 16 to January 25 at 105,000, including 19,246 dead. Thousands more suffered from trench foot, frostbite, and disease. Roughly one in ten U.S. combat casualties during World War II

Soldiers examine a helmet pierced by German bullets.

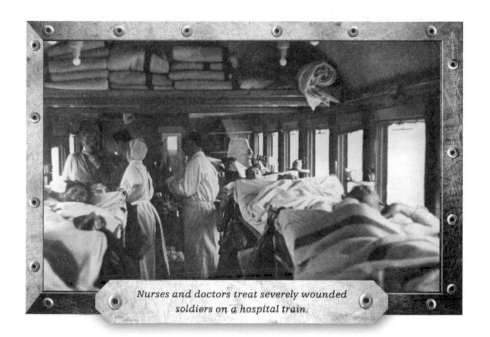

Nurses and doctors treat severely wounded soldiers on a hospital train.

occurred in the bulge, where 600,000 GIs had fought, four times the number of combatants in blue and gray at Gettysburg. More than 23,000 were taken prisoner; most spent the duration in German camps, living on seven hundred calories a day and drinking fake coffee "so foul we used to bathe in it," as one captured officer later recalled. Families of soldiers from the obliterated 106th Infantry Division organized the "Agony Grapevine," conceived by a Pittsburgh lumberman whose son had gone missing on the Schnee Eifel. Volunteers with shortwave radios kept nightly vigils, listening to German propaganda broadcasts that sometimes named captured prisoners.

Of more than sixty thousand wounded and injured, those who had come closest to death often lay wide-eyed on their hospital cots, as one surgeon wrote, "like somebody rescued from the ledge of a skyscraper." Many would need months, if not years, to recover. A wounded officer described a jammed hospital courtyard in March filled with broken men on stretchers. A soldier wrote his parents in Nevada of narrowly surviving a gunfight on January 13, when a German shell scorched past him. "I looked down and my rt. hand was gone. . . . Dad, you'll have to be patient with me until I learn to bowl left-handed."

German losses would be difficult to count with precision, not least because the Americans tended to inflate them. (Patton at times simply made up numbers, or assumed that enemy casualties were tenfold the number of prisoners taken.) A U.S. Army estimate of 120,000 enemy losses in the month following the launch of AUTUMN MIST was surely too high, and Bradley's claim of more than a quarter million was preposterous.

American tanks pass bodies of German soldiers.

One postwar analysis put the figure at 82,000, another at 98,000. The official German history would cite 11,000 dead and 34,000 wounded, with an indeterminate number captured, missing, sick, and injured.

Model's success in extricating much of his force—in late January, Germany still listed 289 divisions, the same number counted by SHAEF on December 10—belied the Reich's true plight. "He bent the bow until it broke," Manteuffel said of the Army Group B commander. German forces in the west had virtually no fuel reserves and only about a third of the ammunition they needed. The Luftwaffe was so feeble that Hitler likened air warfare to "a rabbit hunt." More than seven hundred armored vehicles had been lost in the Ardennes, German manpower reserves were exhausted, and the rail system was so badly battered that as of January 19, all freight shipments were banned except for coal and war matériel. After more than five years of war, four million German soldiers had been killed, wounded, or captured. Hitler professed to find solace in a letter Frederick the Great had written during the Seven Years' War: "I started this war with the most wonderful army in Europe. Today I've got a muck heap."

Patton sensed the kill. "When you catch a carp and put him in the boat," he told reporters, "he flips his tail just before he dies. I think this is the German's last flip." Manteuffel came to the same conclusion. The Battle of the Bulge had left the Germans so enfeebled, he warned, that they henceforth would be capable of fighting only "a corporal's war," a small skirmish. And right he was. The end of this great conflict was in sight.

EPILOGUE

FEW U.S. GENERALS had enhanced their reputations in the Ardennes, except for battle stalwarts like Brigadier General Anthony McAuliffe. An American army that considered itself the offensive spirit incarnate had paradoxically fought best on the defensive. The cautious January counterattack designed by Bradley and Montgomery, with Eisenhower's consent, pushed Germans from the bulge rather than beating them out; though it was intended to "trap the maximum troops in the salient," the effort trapped almost no one. Among top commanders, Patton proved the most distinguished. His remarkable agility in fighting the German Seventh Army, half the Fifth Panzer Army, and portions of the Sixth Panzer Army was best summarized in Bradley's six-word tribute: "One of our great combat leaders."

Winston Churchill sought to repair Anglo-American discord with a gracious speech in the House of Commons.

On January 24, 1945, American soldiers of the 75th Infantry Division march through the forest to cut off the road to St.-Vith.

Speaking of the contest in the Ardennes, he said, "United States troops have done almost all the fighting and have suffered almost all the losses," he said. "They have lost sixty to eighty men for every one of ours." The Battle of the Bulge "is undoubtedly the greatest American battle of the war and will, I believe, be regarded as an ever-famous American victory." To his secretary, the prime minister later remarked that there was "no greater exhibition of power in history than that of the American army fighting the battle of the Ardennes with its left hand and advancing from island to island toward Japan with its right." Montgomery also showed unusual courtesy in notes to Eisenhower and Bradley, "my dear Brad," telling the latter, "What a great honour it has been for me to command such fine troops."

Eisenhower claimed that the German offensive "had in no sense achieved anything decisive." In fact, AUTUMN MIST had hastened the Third Reich's demise. Hitler's preoccupation with the west in late 1944—and the diversion of supplies, armor, and reserves from the east—proved a "godsend for the Red [Russian] Army," in the estimate of one German historian. Half of Germany's fuel production in November and December had supported the Ardennes offensive, and now hundreds of German tanks and assault guns fighting the Russians were immobilized on the Eastern Front for lack of gasoline. By January 20, the massive Soviet force of two million men had torn a hole nearly 350 miles wide from East Prussia to the Carpathian foothills, bypassing or annihilating German defenses. Bound for the Oder River, Stalin's armies would be

Russian soldiers load a Katyusha rocket launcher during their final advance into Berlin.

within fifty miles of Berlin at a time when the Anglo-Americans had yet to reach the Rhine. Here, six hundred miles from the Ardennes, was the greatest consequence of the Battle of the Bulge.

On January 25, 1945, the Western Allies counted 3.7 million soldiers in seventy-three divisions along a 729-mile front, with U.S. forces providing more than two-thirds of that strength. Eisenhower also had almost 18,000 combat aircraft—complemented by air fleets in Italy—and over-whelming dominance in artillery, armor, intelligence, supply, transportation, and the other essentials of modern combat. The Pentagon accelerated the sailing dates of seven U.S. divisions, diverted two others not previously earmarked for Europe, and combed out units in Alaska, Panama, and other quiet theaters where George Marshall, chief of staff of the U.S. Army, believed "plenty of fat meat" could be found. So desperate was the need for rifle-platoon leaders that an emergency school for new lieutenants opened in the Louis XV wing of the Château de Fontainebleau outside Paris, with classes in map reading, patrolling, and camouflage. Many of these students were among the almost 30,000 U.S. enlisted men who received promotions and battlefield commissions during the war. Army draft levies, which had just increased from 60,000 to 90,000 men a month, would jump again in March to 100,000. SHAEF expected the armies in the west to grow to eighty-five divisions by May.

That would have to suffice. Britain had nearly run out of men, and the American replacement pool was described as "almost depleted," with much hard fighting still to come against

Germany and Japan. Eisenhower asked for a hundred thousand marines; he would get none. Patton calculated that victory in western Europe required "twenty more divisions of infantry"; that was a pipe dream. Eisenhower would have to win with the forces now committed to his theater, and no more.

The Battle of the Bulge had affirmed once again that war is never linear, but rather a chaotic, haphazard enterprise of reversal and advance, blunder and enthusiasm, despair and elation. Valor, cowardice, courage—each had been displayed in this spectacle of a marching world. For magnitude and violence, the battle in the Ardennes was unlike any seen before in American history, nor like any to be seen again. Yet as always, even as armies and army groups collided, it was the fates of individual soldiers that drew the eye.

"Everybody shares the same universals—hope, love, humor, faith," Private First Class Richard E. Cowan of the 2nd Infantry Division had written his family in Kansas on December 5, 1944, his twenty-second birthday. Two weeks later, he was dead, killed near Krinkelt after holding off German attackers with a machine gun long enough to cover his comrades' escape. "It is such a bitter dose to have to take," his mother confessed after hearing the news, "and I am not a bit brave about it." Cowan would be awarded the Medal of Honor, one of thirty-two recognizing heroics in the Battle of the Bulge. Like so many thousands of others, he would be interred in one of those two-by-five-by-six-and-a-half-foot graves, along with his last full measure of hope, love, humor, and faith. The marching world marched on.

THE END OF THE WAR

WITH THE end of the Battle of the Bulge, the Western Allies resumed the advance across Europe that had begun on Normandy's beaches more than six months earlier. American, British, Canadian, and French armies pushed from the Ardennes battlefields into Germany, driving toward the valley of the Rhine River, which protected the enemy's heartland like a wide moat.

On March 7, American soldiers unexpectedly found a Rhine bridge still standing at Remagen, a village south of Bonn. Frantic German attempts to blow up the bridge failed, and GIs swept across to the river's eastern bank. In the next several weeks, additional crossings were made to the north and south. By the end of March, combat engineers had built more than a half dozen sturdy bridges across the Rhine, allowing tanks, trucks, and infantrymen to capture several key German cities.

On March 31, 1945, British Field Marshal Bernard Montgomery and Prime Minister Winston Churchill, accompanied by American soldiers, cross the Rhine River to see how the assault on Nazi Germany is progressing.

Allied soldiers march through the Siegfried Line.

In April, American forces surrounded the German industrial center known as the Ruhr Valley. Three hundred thousand enemy soldiers surrendered, and their commander shot himself rather than face capture. The final drive across Germany gained momentum, with American forces sweeping across Bavaria in the south to eventually occupy Austria and part of Czechoslovakia. British and Canadian troops pushed north through the cities of Hanover and Hamburg. Some German towns surrendered without a fight; others resisted and were smashed to rubble.

From the east, Soviet forces encircled Berlin. On April 30, 1945, Adolf Hitler committed suicide in his underground lair. The capital soon was overrun. Surviving German military leaders agreed to the unconditional surrender of all forces still fighting. The capitulation documents were signed at General Eisenhower's headquarters in Reims, France, on May 7. The war in Europe was over. The Third Reich, which Hitler had boasted would endure for a thousand years, had lasted for just twelve, ending with the utter destruction of the German empire and Germany's military occupation by the victorious Allies.

The Queen Elizabeth *sails into New York Harbor with thousands of returning soldiers.*

CHARLES DE GAULLE

GENERAL CHARLES A.J.M. DE GAULLE was the head of the self-proclaimed provisional French government in exile. Prior to France's surrender to Germany on June 22, 1940, de Gaulle had been undersecretary of state for defense. He fled from France to England, where over radio broadcasts he urged French citizens to continue to resist the Germans. He gathered French military personnel already stationed in England into the Free French Forces.

De Gaulle was not wholeheartedly embraced by the Allies. He was excluded from the planning of D-Day, the invasion of Normandy on June 6, 1944, and the U.S. government did not recognize de Gaulle's Free French as a legitimate government, although Churchill was more welcoming. De Gaulle felt these snubs and could be resentful.

De Gaulle arrived in France on June 14, 1944. He addressed a gathering of French citizens in person, and many saw him as a beacon of hope. The Free French troops later marched through liberated Paris. Once Free French Forces could enlist the freed citizens of France, their numbers grew to half a million. They fought together with the Allies in the French countryside and along the border of Germany.

During the battles in the Ardennes region, de Gaulle was unmovable in his demand that the city of Strasbourg on the German border be defended at a time when Allied commanders wanted to pull back west of the city to regroup for a final push against the Germans.

After the war, De Gaulle served as president of France from 1959 to 1969.

CHANGING THE U.S. DRAFT LAWS TO SUPPLY REINFORCEMENTS

THE SELECTIVE SERVICE, the agency of the U.S. government that keeps records of citizens eligible for military service, changed its rules as the war went on in order to enlist more people. The exemption for fathers was abolished: one million would be drafted in 1944–45. The average age of draftees had climbed from twenty-two in 1940 to twenty-six in 1944, and many new privates were over thirty-five. A ban on shipping eighteen-year-olds overseas was removed in August 1944. And a three-page document alerted armed service examiners how to detect draftees who were trying

U.S. Army sergeants examine new recruits.

to dodge their duty by feigning epilepsy, pretending to be bed wetters, or using drugs to speed up their heart rate to mimic tachycardia. Would-be draft dodgers "may shoot or cut off their fingers or toes. . . . Some may put their hands under cars for this purpose."

In December 1944, the American armed forces comprised twelve million, compared with five million for the British, but the need for even more soldiers was great. One million Army troops were now fighting the war on the Pacific front, while the Army Air Forces had requested 130,000 men to fly and maintain the new B-29 bomber, called the Superfortress, beyond the 300,000 workers already building the planes. Almost five million American men had been granted occupational deferments. Many soldiers were being sent back from Europe to work in hard-pressed critical industries, alongside millions of women already working in American factories. In December, 2,500 GIs were sent home to make artillery ammunition and an additional 2,000 to make tires; thousands more went to foundries, toolmakers, and other plants. In late 1944, Congress sensed the approaching end of the war and pressured the U.S. Army chief of staff, General George C. Marshall, to reduce Army manpower so that the production of consumer goods, from toasters to Buicks, could resume on the home front.

U.S. battle casualties in Europe had doubled from October to November to 2,000 a day; on December 7, the figure hit 3,000. The trench foot epidemic caused nonbattle casualties to also double in November, to 56,000. Consequently, even as the last of the U.S. Army's eighty-nine divisions prepared for deployment overseas, and even though more than 300,000 individual replacement troops had arrived since D-Day, General Omar Bradley's 12th Army Group reported in December that every division already in the theater was below its authorized strength. "The life expectancy of a junior officer in combat was twelve days before he was hit and evacuated," Bradley asserted. Lieutenant General George Patton wrote in his diary on December 3, "Our situation is bad; 11,000 short in an army of three armored divisions and six infantry divisions."

U.S. WINTER BATTLE CLOTHING

IN THE BEST of circumstances, supplying soldiers with clothing was a logistical struggle. Much of the clothing for American troops was made in the United States, carried by ship to an Allied port in Europe, and delivered by train, truck, or air to the front lines.

U.S. troops in Europe in the winter of 1944–45 suffered severe shortages of warm clothing. Some supplies were slow to arrive, and others had to be moved far from the front lines to avoid capture by the Germans. Every day, tons of clothing and supplies were delivered to the armies. Even so, it was not until late February 1945 that sufficient stores were in place for the troops in what had been a brutally cold winter.

The army's approach to issuing clothing for troops in winter combat was based on layering: pieces could be added or removed depending on the weather. The fully supplied American soldier—and there were not many of them—would have had the following winter battle clothing:

- Field jacket with a pile fabric liner (The M-1943 jacket was developed for World War II soldiers and had the advantage of being wind-resistant as well as big enough to wear layers underneath.)
- Hood
- Wool shirt
- Heavy wool overcoat
- Raincoat or British-made poncho, which could also be used as a ground sheet
- Combat boots
- Arctic or ski socks
- Overshoes
- Insoles for boots

- Field cap
- Trigger-finger shell mittens with liners
- Sweater
- Scarf
- Wool underwear
- Sleeping bag
- Blanket
- Ground sheet

Soldiers on the front lines had to camouflage their positions. Because of shortages, at least five thousand white mattress covers were made into hooded camouflage suits. Tanks in snowy terrain were painted white.

To add to the drain on all resources, the Allies were responsible for providing food and other supplies to civilians in the towns and villages they moved through, as well as to prisoners of war and the Free French troops who were aiding the Allies.

A U.S. supply and transport convoy snakes through narrow tracks in the Ardennes.

RADIO COMMUNICATIONS ON THE BATTLEFIELD

PORTABLE RADIO SETS provided a common method of communication among groups of soldiers on the European battle fronts. (Others included written messages delivered by runners and field telephones connected by wire.) There was a radio in every tank, sometimes more than one, and every platoon had its own radio. The most powerful radios could transmit voice over one hundred miles and Morse code over several hundred miles, but most had much shorter range.

Radios were also used to communicate with spies and with civilians behind enemy lines who supported the Allies. People had code names, specific times to call, and designated frequencies to tune in to. Radio operators sat over radio boxes with headphones on, turning the dials, listening for information. Of course, the enemy could listen in on radio frequencies also. Radio chatter often tipped one off to the other side's plans.

You can make a crystal radio much like the ones used in World War II at home. Several good step-by-step directions are available online. Put the words "crystal radio" in a search engine, or go to open.edu and search for "Building a crystal radio set," or see wikihow.com/Make-a-Crystal-Radio.

TRACKS, TANKS, AND PLANES AT THE BATTLE OF THE BULGE

HALF-TRACKS

HALF-TRACKS were particularly useful in winter warfare. With regular tires in front and tracks in back, these all-terrain vehicles could climb steep hillsides, stay operational in mud and on ice, and plow through heavy snow. They resembled a half truck/half tank and had mounted guns for self-defense. For the most part, half-tracks were not assault vehicles.

The American M2 half-track car was developed after the success of the French Citroen half-track. After World War I, it became clear that armies could no longer depend on horses and carts to transport troops in rough terrain or bad weather. The new armies would have to be able to move many soldiers quickly. The half-track car had a crew of two and could transport seven soldiers and their gear. It was agile enough to be used for reconnaissance. To keep it light enough to move quickly, the developers gave up heavy armor—though it still weighed nine tons, it could travel up to forty miles per hour. The shell was thin and the top was open, leaving passengers and crew vulnerable to explosives and machine-gun fire. By the end of the war, 13,500 M2 half-tracks had been manufactured in the United States and Canada and delivered to the Allied forces.

Demand increased for a vehicle that could carry more troops. The American M3 half-track was the answer. It could carry thirteen soldiers: a crew of three and a ten-person rifle squad. It could also serve as a weapons platform, equipment carrier, and antitank gun tow, and was used to carry the wounded to hospitals in the rear. More than forty-one thousand were made for service in the war.

The Germans also used half-track vehicles. The German SdKfz 251 was developed to keep up with fast-moving panzers. Many versions of it

were in place during the war, including one that used infrared search-lights for night fighting.

FULL-TRACKS

SOME FULL-TRACK VEHICLES, such as the M29 Weasel, were specially
designed to be light and fast to carry small groups of commando troops to the front, deliver supplies, or serve as ambulances or radio command centers. These tanks had to be light enough to be carried in an airplane and sturdy enough to survive being dropped by parachutes. The M29 could carry up to four people or 1,200 pounds of materials. In the winter, it could be used to pull sleds of supplies.

After the war, M29s were used in the Arctic and Antarctic to support explorers and scientists.

An American Sherman tank

TANKS

THE AMERICAN M4 SHERMAN TANK was
a staple of World War II, used by U.S., British, Canadian, and Free French armies. It was a nimble tank, able to climb steep ravines, navigate through snow and mud, and move at about twenty-five miles per hour. German tanks, like the Mark V Panther and the Mark VI Tiger, were heavier.

They carried more powerful guns than the M4, but the sheer number of M4s eventually overwhelmed the German tank force.

PLANES

THE P–47 THUNDERBOLT was a staple of World War II. It boasted eight Browning machine guns and could carry up to 2,500 pounds of bombs or ten rockets. Although large, the plane was excellent at diving, so pilots could accurately take out targets. P-47 units destroyed 86,000 railway cars, 9,000 locomotives, 6,000 armored fighting vehicles, and 68,000 trucks between D-Day and the end of the war in Europe.

The Piper L-4 was a small light plane mainly used for reconnaissance. It held a pilot and a scout, who radioed back the location of enemy units and artillery. Nicknamed the Grasshopper because it was nimble and could land and take off quickly, the L-4 was also used for courier services and to deliver officers and doctors to and from the front.

The German Luftwaffe gathered more than 2,400 aircraft to support the offensive in the Ardennes, including the heavily armored Heinkel He 111 bombers and the lightning-fast Messerschmitt 109 fighters. Even though the mountain fog and snow during the Battle of the Bulge precluded the use of significant airpower, the Germans managed to fly as many as 1,200 sorties on some days.

The P-47 Thunderbolt fighter-bomber was a versatile plane during the war. The P-47D flew in Europe; the P-47N, a similar model pictured above, flew in the Pacific theater.

NAPALM AND POISON GAS

NAPALM

NAPALM BOMBS were developed to ignite easily on contact, bursting into flames and destroying people and vegetation, burning into caves and bunkers, and destroying tanks and other heavily armored vehicles. It was named for its original ingredients: naphthenic acid and palmitic acid. Napalm is a gel; its thick texture causes it to stick to the surfaces it lands on as it ignites. Perfected by a professor at Harvard University, Louis Fieser, napalm was used as a weapon during World War II and in wars to follow. Because of the extreme burns it causes, it is now against international law to target civilians with napalm bombs. Napalm was used in incendiary bombs and flamethrowers in World War II.

POISON GAS ON THE BATTLEFIELD

BOTH ALLIED AND AXIS countries had stockpiles of poison gases. The fear of their use was very real because gases had been used as weapons in World War I. A U.S. Army manual informed soldiers that if they were subjected to the nerve gas soman, they could be dead in as little as two minutes. Another kind of gas, called mustard gas, caused severe pain and burns. Most likely because of fear of reprisals, neither side used poison gases on the battlefield in World War II.

WINTER TAKES ITS TOLL

COLD INJURIES plagued the troops in the winter of 1944–45. Those serving in Europe were often wet and quite cold. Although the armed forces had learned a great deal about winter combat injuries during cold-weather fighting in Italy earlier in the war, lack of supplies did not allow soldiers to always take proper precautions.

Four particular conditions were prevalent during the Battle of the Bulge: trench foot, frostbite, hypothermia, and snow blindness.

TRENCH FOOT is caused by wearing wet boots and socks for too long and is made worse by standing for long periods of time in the cold. Symptoms include swollen white or gray feet and feet that feel numb or prickly. Skin may turn blue, red, or black. Sometimes infections occur. The pain is extreme and can last a long time. Soldiers with trench foot were often evacuated and faced weeks or months of rehabilitation.

FROSTBITE occurs when not only the skin is frozen (frostnip), but also the tissue under the skin. This very serious condition is easy to spot but difficult to treat. A frostbitten limb looks dead; it is a waxy pale blue or yellow color and feels cold and heavy. The most severe danger in a frostbite condition comes from warming a limb only to have it freeze again, so most World War II frostbite victims were evacuated to a hospital far from the front lines before being warmed up.

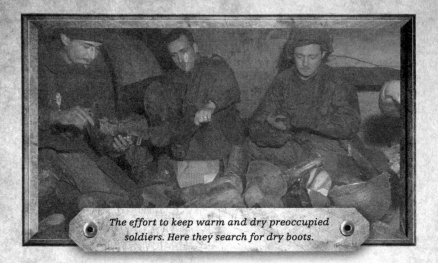

*The effort to keep warm and dry preoccupied
soldiers. Here they search for dry boots.*

HYPOTHERMIA is a dangerous lowering in body temperature, a condition that occurs when a body loses heat faster than it can generate it. It occurs when a body's core temperature drops from a normal level (about 98 degrees Fahrenheit) to 95 degrees or lower. Many soldiers did not have sufficient dry clothing—or enough clothing at all—to keep them warm. Hypothermia is potentially fatal; exposure to wind or cold makes the body lose heat much faster. To conserve heat, the body slows down in extreme cold. One's heart rate decreases, breathing slows, and, therefore, the brain slows down too. This can cause confusion and weariness. Sometimes, soldiers with hypothermia were mistaken for dead.

SNOW BLINDNESS, also called sunburn of the eye, is caused by looking out at snowfields on very sunny days. It is most common in high altitudes, where the snow reflects the ultraviolet rays and can be intense enough to burn the cornea in the eye. Eyelids swell and eyes become red, teary, and feel gritty. Although the condition is usually temporary, it requires that eyes remain closed, usually covered with patches, for one or two days.

"KILROY WAS HERE"

"KILROY WAS HERE" is a graffiti drawing that American soldiers left as they passed through European towns. The figure showed up on walls, sidewalks, abandoned tanks, and latrines. Kilroy was a positive figure—meant to show anyone who saw it that the victorious army had passed by, that, the Americans were here. There are several myths about the origin of the figure, but none can be proved. The most common theory attributes the phrase to James Kilroy, an American shipyard inspector during the war, who is said to have scrawled the phrase on new ship bulkheads to show that he had inspected the rivets.

British soldiers drew a figure called Chad. Chad was used to complain about shortages or express fantasy wishes. Above his face were the words "Wot no . . ." ("What? No . . .") that could be finished with "hot water," "caviar," "beer," or anything else the graffiti artist was longing for.

KILROY WAS HERE

HORSES, MULES, AND DOGS OF WAR

Blanketed German troop horses at rest.

ONLY ONE-FIFTH OF the German army was mechanized during World War II. In 1944, of 264 German combat divisions, only 42 were fully reliant on engine power. The country did not have sufficient oil resources from which to draw fuel for tanks and trucks and jeeps. So the army relied on horses and mules to pull cannon and other artillery, supply sleds, and mobile hospital tents; to provide the muscle for removing debris from roads and trails; and to carry soldiers through all manner of terrains. The horses required care and a constant source of food. Supply wagons carried rations for the troops and the animals. Mules were used to haul; horses were used both to haul and to carry riders.

The United States had a few units during World War II that included horses. These served primarily in Italy, purchasing horses locally instead of shipping them from the United States.

Dogs were trained for battle in several roles. They were sentries, scouts, and messengers. There were rescue dogs and mine-detecting dogs. Soldiers serving in the Ardennes recalled hearing German sentry dogs in the darkness.

Occasionally units adopted stray dogs, but the conditions during the Battle of the Bulge were so extreme that there was usually not enough shelter or food for pet animals.

An American soldier sleeps while his dog stands sentry. This photograph was taken in 1945 as the Allies fought to take the island of Iwo Jima from the Japanese Empire.

SIGNAL CORPS

MOST OF THE IMAGES in this book were taken by photographers of the U.S. Army Signal Corps. The Signal Corps was a branch of the U.S. Army that served both the Army Ground Forces and the Army Air Forces. After the attack on Pearl Harbor in December 1941 and the entry of the United States into the war, the Signal Corps had to expand rapidly. It gathered men and women from Hollywood, workers at electronics and telephone companies, and groups of pigeon breeders and trainers. Several famous Hollywood directors went to war to record the troops' actions. Some Signal Corps soldiers worked in the United States at several training facilities

Soldiers in the Army Signal Corps were just behind infantrymen on the front lines. Their photographs and film footage informed people at home and have provided invaluable primary source documentation about the war.

and in communications offices around Washington, D.C. Others were assigned to troop divisions and central communications centers in Europe and the Pacific.

The commitment of 16.1 million U.S. troops in World War II and the integration necessary among all the nations fighting on each front meant that communication was essential. The Signal Corps rallied more than 350,000 uniformed men and women to create training films for soldiers and newsreels to be shown in American movie theaters, to disseminate lessons in using crystal radios, to set up communication systems between the front and the rear of troop movements and battles, and to coordinate communication among air, ground, and naval units. During the course of the war, the Signal Corps refined the use of radar to detect incoming aircraft and developed code-breaking machines that tackled enemy messages.

More than five thousand WACs, members of the Women's Army Corps, served in the Signal Corps both at home and abroad. Also among the Signal Corps were Native American "code talkers." These men spoke a language that few others knew and that was largely unwritten. They relayed messages to other Native Americans, who would translate the messages for their English-speaking officers. Anyone listening who was not a native speaker would not understand the message.

Communications systems were built to connect Washington and London with General Eisenhower's traveling headquarters, and with offices in all Allied and neutral countries. More than ten thousand men and women monitored radio communications from around the world and passed on intelligence.

Another major responsibility of the Signal Corps, specifically the Army Pictorial Service, was to film and photograph combat operations. The corps supplied pictures to the news media, ensuring that the public had a dramatic visual sense of what was happening. Most members of the corps were trained first as soldiers and then as photographers, so they carried guns and cameras. Many of the cameras these soldiers used were purchased from or donated by private citizens, since there was not enough time to mass-produce them.

WEAPONS USED BY INFANTRY

INFANTRY, men on the ground, were the backbone of the Allied strength and success during the Battle of the Bulge. The landscape made it difficult to mobilize many tanks, and the weather delayed the launching of bombers and reconnaissance planes. Infantrymen carried weapons that ranged from knives and pistols to mortars.

Here are some classes of weapons.

KNIVES

Specially designed combat knives were meant for close fighting. They could also be used to open ration tins and for other mundane tasks.

PISTOLS

Although not effective in intense battle, pistols were carried by many soldiers. The FP-45 Liberator was dropped into enemy-occupied territory to be used by resistance forces.

BOLT-ACTION RIFLES

Accurate to a half mile, these rifles were the standard issue at the beginning of the war. But they were cumbersome. A soldier had to reload after each shot and carry a good quantity of ammunition. Bolt-action rifles were soon replaced by newer semiautomatic rifles. Some rifles were fitted with magnifying telescope sights and used by snipers.

SEMIAUTOMATIC RIFLES

The semiautomatic rifle was the next refinement to bolt-action rifles. They were self-loading and therefore allowed the shooter to advance, keeping his target in sight.

SUBMACHINE GUNS

Although these could fire fast, they were not especially accurate.

ANTITANK WEAPONS

These rockets could be fired by infantrymen. They launched a hollow warhead that could pierce steel tanks. The bazooka was one used by the U.S. infantry.

FLAMETHROWERS

Although the safest way to use a flamethrower was to mount it on a tank, the weapon could also be carried. The combustible ingredient was stored in a backpack and shot through a nozzle. The burning fuel was sufficient to roust the enemy from entrenched positions. See also the description of napalm on page 212.

HAND GRENADES

These were easy to deploy and inexpensive to make and were used by the thousands.

MORTARS

Mortars were sometimes used from trenches. The weapon was a long tube; one end rested on the ground, while the other was angled upward and was supported by bipod or tripod feet. Soldiers didn't have to poke their heads above their trenches to fire it. The mortar delivered its ammunition in a high arc, so it could reach beyond tanks, over trees and hedges, and behind buildings. Mortars could also shoot smoke bombs to cover infantry actions and light shells to give illumination at night. They were easy to carry, set up, and take care of on the battlefield.

NUMBERS TELL PART OF THE STORY

THE BATTLE OF THE BULGE AT A GLANCE

December 16, 1944–January 25, 1945

U.S. NUMBERS

600,000 GIs fought in the Ardennes

19,246 soldiers died

23,000 GIs taken prisoner

More than 60,000 GIs wounded or injured

One in 10 U.S. combat casualties during World War II occurred during the Battle of the Bulge

GERMAN NUMBERS*

250,000 men fought on the front lines

11,000 dead

34,000 wounded

WORLD WAR II AT A GLANCE

How long the war lasted...2,174 days

Countries involved in World War II.................................61

Americans who served in uniform....................................16.1 million

United Kingdom citizens who served in uniform................5.9 million

Canadians who served in uniform....................................1.1 million

Average time each U.S. serviceman spent overseas.............16 months

Bombs dropped by Allies...3.4 million tons

Airplanes that the U.S. 8th Air Force shot down................6,098

Americans unaccounted for at the end of the war...............73,000

Estimated number of GIs buried in Europe.......................25,000

U.S. military dead...405,399

U.S. civilian dead..1,700[†]

U.S. soldiers wounded.....................................671,278

U.K. military dead..383,600

U.K. civilian dead..67,100

U.K. soldiers wounded......................................326,000

Canadian military dead.....................................23,000

Canadian soldiers wounded................................54,000

Soviet military dead...8.8–10.7 million

Soviet civilian dead...13–15 million

Soviet soldiers wounded....................................14,915,517

German military dead..5,533,000

German civilian dead..1,067,000–3,267,000

German soldiers wounded...................................6,035,000

European Jews killed during the Holocaust...........6 million

Japanese dead in Hiroshima bombing.................90,000–120,000[‡]

Japanese dead in Nagasaki bombing..................60,000–80,000[‡]

Deaths worldwide...60 million[§]

[*]German losses are difficult to count with precision. These numbers are taken from the official German history.

[†]1,500 American citizens were living in Japan at the time of the declaration of war. They died in internment camps. About 180 U.S. citizens were living in Germany and also died in captivity. At Pearl Harbor, 68 civilians died.

[‡]Many more died later of diseases caused by radiation poisoning.

[§]27,600 every day of the war, 1,150 every hour, or 19 every minute.

BATTLE OF THE BULGE TIMELINE

DECEMBER 11, 1944
Adolf Hitler unveils his plan for HERBSTNEBEL, or AUTUMN MIST, to his field commanders.

DECEMBER 16, 1944
Null Tag, or Zero Day: German forces cross the German border into Belgium in the initial attack.

DECEMBER 17, 1944
More than eighty Allied prisoners of war are massacred at Malmédy.

DECEMBER 18, 1944
Colonel Hurley E. Fuller captured near Clervaux.

DECEMBER 19, 1944
The Germans capture more than seven thousand surrounded U.S. troops in the Schnee Eifel.

DECEMBER 21, 1944
The siege of Bastogne begins.

DECEMBER 22, 1944
The Germans capture St.-Vith. Lieutenant General von Lüttwitz delivers a message requesting surrender to Brigadier General McAuliffe, who replies, "Nuts!"

DECEMBER 25, 1944
The Allies stop the Germans five miles east of the Meuse River.

DECEMBER 26, 1944
Lieutenant General George Patton's troops, under the command of Lieutenant Colonel Creighton Abrams, arrive to reinforce Bastogne.

JANUARY 1, 1945
The reinforced British 6th Airborne and 53rd Infantry Divisions move against the western tip of the German advance; Germany launches Operation BODENPLATTE, or BASEPLATE, with strikes against airfields in the Netherlands and Belgium.

JANUARY 3, 1945
The U.S. First Army attacks the Germans' northern flank in the bulge; German Panzer divisions begin to withdraw from the front lines toward the interior of the bulge.

JANUARY 12, 1945
The German offensive into France is stopped thirteen miles from Strasbourg.

JANUARY 25, 1945
The Germans are pushed back to the line they held before AUTUMN MIST. The Battle of the Bulge ends.

GLOSSARY

ABSCESS–a painful swelling filled with pus

ADJUTANT–staff officer who assists a commanding officer

ARMOR–mechanized units of military forces and vehicles, such as tanks

AWOL–away from military duties without permission, from "Absent Without Leave"

BATTERY–an artillery grouping with six or more guns

BATTLE DRESS–standard uniform worn into combat

BLITZ–an intensive military aerial campaign

BULKHEAD–a structure designed to withstand pressure

BUNKER–a reinforced chamber, often underground, meant to protect inhabitants

CALIBRATE–to adjust precisely

CAMPAIGN–a series of operations in a war

CAUSEWAY–a raised road above wet ground or water

COMBAT ENGINEER–a team member who constructs floating bridges, places and detonates explosives, constructs defensive positions, and detects mines

CORDITE–a smokeless gunpowder

CULVERT–a drain

DEPLOY–to place in a battle formation

DEPRIVATION–lacking the necessities of life, such as food and shelter

DRUMFIRE–artillery firing continuously, sounding like a drumroll

ENTRENCH–to dig in

ENTRENCHING TOOL–a folding shovel used to dig trenches

FLANK–area to the side of a formation

FRONT–the line between two armies

FRONTAGE–the length of the line between armies

FUEL DUMP–a storage location for quantities of gasoline

FÜHRER–leader, the title assumed by Adolf Hitler

FUSILLADE–shots fired simultaneously or in rapid succession

GESTAPO–German secret police organization

"GIVE NO QUARTER"–to show no mercy or make no concessions

GUN CARRIAGE–the frame that supports an artillery piece, usually with wheels to allow the gun to be positioned precisely

HALF-TRACK–a vehicle with wheels in the front and a circular chain-drive system in the back

INCENDIARY–a weapon designed to start fires

INTERDICT–to destroy, damage, or cut off an enemy's supply line

INTER–to put a dead body in a grave in the ground or in a tomb

JACKBOOTS–military boots that extend above the knee

KILOMETER–unit of distance equal to 0.62 of a mile

LIME–a white powder made from limestone, mixed with water to make whitewash

LOGGERHEADS–(at) in a state of disagreement, accompanied by some anger or frustration

LOGISTICIANS–military personnel responsible for the procurement and delivery of matériel and troops

LUFTWAFFE–aerial warfare branch of the German military during World War II

LUNGE–a sudden forward rush

MASTERSTROKE–a superior performance or move

MATÉRIEL–military equipment and supplies

MECHANIZE–to equip with tanks and other armored vehicles

MOTORCADE–a procession of vehicles

MUSTER–to assemble for military inspection, to gather

NAPALM–a gel used to set targets on fire

PANTHER–a medium-size German tank used in World War II

PANZER–the German word for "tank"

PARLEY–a conference with an enemy

PAYBOOK–a record book listing pay received for duty

PILLBOX–a small, low concrete fortification that houses machine guns and antitank weapons

PINCH BAR–a metal tool similar to a crowbar

PROBE–military action intended to get information about enemy defenses

RADIAL–arranged in straight lines from a central point

RADIUM–a metallic element used in materials that light up

RAIL CUT–a path cut through high ground for train tracks

REAR ECHELON–military headquarters located far from the front, usually concerned with supplies and administration

REAR GUARD–soldiers charged with protecting the rear of a fighting group

RECONNAISSANCE–an exploratory survey of enemy territory

SALIENT–an outward bulge in a line of military attack

SALLY–the act of rushing forward from a defensive position

SALVO–a simultaneous discharge of guns

SECTOR–a portion of a military front of operation

SENTRIES–guards

SERENDIPITY–good luck not sought

SHALE–easily split rock formed from layers of clay or silt

SHOCK TROOPS–troops chosen for offensive work because of their training, skills, and morale

SIDEARM–a weapon, such as a revolver, worn at the side or in a belt

SPAN–the spread between two supports

SPOILING ATTACK–an attack mounted on an advancing enemy in order to disrupt its activities

SS–abbreviation for the German *Schutzstaffel*, a unit initially formed to guard Hitler and later expanded to handle intelligence, security, and mass extermination

STRAFE–to fire at close range, usually from low-flying aircraft

SULFURIC ACID–a strong, colorless, corrosive acid

TERRAIN–the ground or geographic area

THERMITE GRENADE–a thrown device meant to start fires at its destination

TNT–a flammable toxic compound used in explosives

ULTRA–the Allied intelligence project whose members specialized in decoding intercepted German messages encrypted by electrical cipher machines

VECTOR–to guide in flight using radioed compass directions

WEST WALL–the German name for the Siegfried Line, the defensive forts and obstacles built by Germany along its border with France

WHEELING MOVEMENT–a movement in a circular or curving direction

PLACES TO VISIT

THE SCALE of World War II was such that nearly every town and city in Europe was affected, and most have their own commemoration of the war, small or large. Many communities in the United States have erected monuments as well. Whether it's a monument to the military men and women who died in the effort or to the civilians who supported and endured the war efforts, a preserved battlefield or headquarters, or a museum, the legacy of the war remains present today. Here are only a small number of those places that commemorate soldiers who fought in the Battle of the Bulge, both in Europe and in the United States.

EUROPE

GEORGE S. PATTON'S GRAVE

Luxembourg American Cemetery

Hamm, Luxembourg

abmc.gov/cemeteries-memorials/europe/luxembourg-american-cemetery

AMERICAN GI STATUE

Honoring the liberation of Clervaux, Luxembourg

The text on one of the plaques reads,

> *To our liberators*
> *1944–1945*
> *They gave us back our freedom*

MARDASSON MEMORIAL

Bastogne, Belgium

The huge star-shaped monument is guarded by an eagle. Its plaque reads,

> *May this eagle always symbolize the sacrifices and heroism*
> *of the 101st Airborne Division and all its attached units.*
> *December 1944–January 1945*

The new Bastogne War Museum is next to the memorial.

ALSO OF INTEREST:

BRIGADIER GENERAL MCAULIFFE MONUMENT

At a crossroads in the town center
Bastogne, Belgium

BASTOGNE BARRACKS

Brigadier General Anthony McAuliffe's underground cellar office is preserved here in a still-active military barracks.

BATTLE OF THE BULGE ROAD TRIP ITINERARY

This Web site outlines a road trip that traces Lieutenant Colonel Joachim Peiper's invasion route from Liège to La Gleize and includes monuments, restored tanks left behind by the Germans, and a cemetery. losapos.com/battle_of_the_bulge_peiper

UNITED STATES

BATTLE OF THE BULGE MEMORIAL
ARLINGTON NATIONAL CEMETERY

Arlington, Virginia

Inscribed on the white marble stone are the words,

> *To World War II American soldiers who fought in the Battle of the Bulge—*
> *The greatest land battle in the history of the United States Army.*

BATTLE OF THE BULGE MEMORIAL

Wolfe's Pond Park

Staten Island, New York

An inscription at the base of the granite columns reads,

> *This is undoubtedly the greatest battle of the War and will, I believe, be*
> *regarded as an ever famous American Victory.*
> —Sir Winston Churchill, addressing the House of Commons, 1945

The granite wall that half circles two tall columns contains the shoulder-patch logos of each of the forty-five units that fought in the battle.

WORLD WAR II MUSEUMS AND MONUMENTS

IN ADDITION to the places listed above, which are specific to the Battle of the Bulge, there are numerous museums and monuments dedicated to the history of World War II and to the memory of the men and women who fought and civilians who died.

NATIONAL WORLD WAR II MEMORIAL

1750 Independence Avenue SW

Washington, D.C.

nps.gov/nwwm

NATIONAL WORLD WAR II MUSEUM

945 Magazine Street

New Orleans, LA

nationalww2museum.org

CANADIAN WAR MUSEUM

1 Vimy Place

Ottawa, Ontario

warmuseum.ca

IMPERIAL WAR MUSEUM LONDON

Lambeth Road

London, England

iwm.org.uk

UNITED STATES HOLOCAUST MEMORIAL MUSEUM

100 Raoul Wallenberg Place SW

Washington, D.C.

ushmm.org

FOR MORE INFORMATION

BOOKS:

Adams, Simon. *Eyewitness Books: World War II*. New York: DK Publications, 2004.

Ambrose, Stephen E. *The Good Fight: How World War II Was Won*. New York: Atheneum Books for Young Readers, 2001.

Atkinson, Rick. *D-Day: The Invasion of Normandy, 1944*. New York: Henry Holt and Company, 2014.

Bachrach, Susan D. *Tell Them We Remember: The Story of the Holocaust*. Boston: Little, Brown Books for Young Readers, 1994.

Birkner, Michael J. *Dwight D. Eisenhower*. Danbury, CT: Children's Press, 2005.

Bull, Stephen. *World War II Winter and Mountain Warfare Tactics*. Oxford, UK: Osprey Publishing, 2013.

Evans, A. A., and David Gibbons. *The Illustrated Timeline of World War II*. New York: Rosen Publishing Group, 2012.

Fein, Eric. *Vehicles of World War II*. North Mankato, MN: Capstone Press, 2014.

Gitlin, Martin. *George S. Patton: World War II General & Military Innovator*. Edina, MN: ABDO Publishing Company, 2010.

Hynson, Colin. *World War II: A Primary Source History*. New York: Gareth Stevens, Inc., 2006.

Martin, Chris. *World War II Book of Lists*. Stroud, UK: The History Press, 2011.

Nicholson, Dorinda Makanaonalani. *Remember World War II: Kids Who Survived Tell Their Stories*. Washington, D.C.: National Geographic Children's Books, 2005.

Oleksy, Walter. *Military Leaders of World War II*. New York: Facts on File, 1994.

Rice, Earle, Jr. *World War II: Strategic Battles in Europe*. San Diego, CA: Lucent Books, 1999.

ONLINE:

The United States Army
army.mil/botb

The United States Department of Defense 60th Anniversary page
defense.gov/home/specials/bulge/index.html

British Broadcasting Corporation
bbc.co.uk/schools/primaryhistory/world_war2

Public Broadcasting Service
pbs.org/wgbh/americanexperience/features/introduction/bulge-introduction

AN INTERVIEW WITH
RICK ATKINSON

What did you want to be when you grew up?

Until I was a senior in high school, I thought I wanted to be an Army officer, like my father and my uncle. I'd grown up on Army posts, and it was the world I knew.

When did you realize you wanted to be a writer?

When I was in high school, several fine teachers helped me to see that I had some writing talent. But it wasn't until I started working at a newspaper, when I was twenty-three, that I thought I could make a living at it.

What's your favorite childhood memory?

Oh, certainly living in some great places—Idaho, San Francisco, and Hawaii, among others—with my family.

As a young person, who did you look up to most?

Probably my father.

What was your favorite thing about school?

I really liked social studies and English. I was a pretty un-talented math and science student.

What book is on your nightstand now?

I'm reading Phil Klay's *Redeployment*, which just won the National Book Award for fiction. And I have a towering stack of books on the American Revolution.

How did you celebrate publishing your first book?

It was 1989, and I don't really remember celebrating. When

I finished *writing* the book, in 1988, I took my family to Hawaii on vacation. My kids were three and five.

Where do you write your books?

I have a big, comfortable office on the second floor of my house in Washington, D.C. The windows look into Rock Creek Park.

Have you always been interested in history? If so, what sparked your interest in history as a kid?

I think every kid should see history as the biggest, most extraordinary story ever written, with heroes, villains, and ordinary people caught in huge events. That's how I saw it.

What fascinated you about D-Day and World War II?

Because I was born in Germany and have lived in Europe for two extended periods, the war has always mesmerized me. June 6, 1944, was probably the most dramatic day for America and Britain in the war.

How has your experience covering recent wars as a journalist changed how you write and think about World War II?

When I was a journalist in Berlin in the mid-1990s, I recognized that the American role in the liberation of Europe really was a drama in three acts: Africa, Italy, and Western Europe. That gave me the idea of writing a trilogy, with exactly that architecture. Having spent time with soldiers in places like Iraq and Somalia, I think I have a vivid sense of what they endure.

Have you visited the Ardennes? What was the experience like?

I've been to the Ardennes, in Belgium and Luxembourg, four or five times. It remains wild and a bit spooky, not greatly changed from the landscape that existed in 1944.

What would you like people to remember about the Battle of the Bulge?

This was a struggle under absolutely awful conditions—

terrible cold, deep snow, a ferocious and desperate enemy, and a dreadful sense of shock since almost everyone had assumed that the war was all but over. Yet American soldiers managed to pull themselves together to stop the German offensive and thwart Hitler's plan.

Do you have a favorite World War II historical figure?

I've lived with General Dwight Eisenhower for more than fifteen years as I've written about World War II, and my admiration for him has only increased. I'm also deeply taken by Generals Ted Roosevelt Jr. and Lucian Truscott Jr., both of whom are in all three volumes of my trilogy. They're great fighting men and natural combat leaders, but they're also intelligent, literate, and sensitive souls.

What would you like readers to take away from your books?

I'd like readers to feel a sense of resolve that the world must never go through the kind of ordeal it went through from 1939 to 1945. It was the greatest catastrophe in human history—over 70 million dead.

What challenges do you face in the writing process, and how do you overcome them?

Writing big historical books is one challenge after another, from trying to sift through mountains of source material to making judgments about what really happened. Perhaps the biggest challenge is to try to bring to life events that happened many years ago.

If you could live in any historical period, which one would you choose?

I was born a few years after World War II ended, but I've never really regretted not being part of my parents' generation. I've always been intrigued by the American Revolution, and I think living in the 1770s and 1780s must have been extraordinary.

If you could travel anywhere in the world, where would you go and what would you do?

I've been to many parts of the world, and I keep trying to see the parts I've not visited. I've never been to China and would very much like to visit soon. I would do mostly what tourists do, but I'd like to get out into some of the remote parts of western China.

Do you ever get writer's block? What do you do to get back on track?

Knock on wood, I don't get writer's block. I keep a sign next to my desk that reads: "Get on with it." That's my creed for most things in life. Get on with it.

What would you do if you ever stopped writing?

Someday, if I'm lucky enough to live to be my father's age—he's ninety now—I will indeed stop writing. Then I can do what I would most like to do: just read.

What would your readers be most surprised to learn about you?

I'm a passionate gardener. There's nothing I like better than playing in the dirt.

DISCUSSION QUESTIONS

THE EUROPEAN THEATER; STAKING EVERYTHING ON ONE CARD; THE SMALL SOLUTION; "NOT TO BE ALTERED" (PAGES 1–20)

- What event precipitated the beginning of WWII?
- What event started the Allied efforts to defeat the Germans in Europe?
- What was Hitler's plan to regain control of the war in Europe in December 1944?
- Why did Hitler's senior commanders object to his "large solution"?
- What was the "small solution" they preferred?
- What were the motivations behind Hitler's plan? Explain.

THE SUPREME COMMANDER; "I STILL HAVE NINE DAYS"; THE ARDENNES: "IT HAS BEEN VERY QUIET UP HERE ..." (PAGES 21–38)

- What was General Eisenhower's strategic plan for defeating Germany?
- How did Churchill and senior British officers react to his plan?
- What was the key problem the Allies faced in carrying out their plans to defeat Germany?
- What signs of a German offensive did the Allies miss or misinterpret? What contributed to this intelligence failure?
- How prepared were the U.S. troops in the Ardennes for a German attack?

THE PLAN WAS FIXED; THE GERMANS' FINAL ASSEMBLY AREA; "NOTHING TO REPORT" (PAGES 39–45)

- What was Hitler's final plan to reach Antwerp?
- Why did the Germans consider the invasion in the Ardennes to be a "holy task"?

- On the eve of battle, what indications were there that the Americans were overconfident?

THIS HAUNTED PLATEAU; THE NORTH; "MUCH HAPPENING OUT THERE" (PAGES 49-66)

- What did Field Marshal Rundstedt mean when he said before the battle, "Everything is at stake" (p. 50)?
- How did SS Lieutenant Colonel Joachim Peiper's devotion to Hitler and Germany lead to numerous instances of battlefield barbarism and atrocities?
- Why was the battle of Elsenborn Ridge significant? What contributed to the Americans' ability to hold the line there?
- Why did the Germans shift their offensive to the south?

THE SOUTH; THE CENTER (PAGES 67-84)

- Although the Germans decisively defeated the 110th Infantry, how did the Americans impact Hitler's Autumn Mist plan?
- What Allied decisions contributed to Germany's relative success near the Schnee Eifel?

"ALL OF US, WITHOUT EXCEPTION, WERE ASTONISHED"; THE LAST GERMAN AIRBORNE OPERATION; SOWING HYSTERIA ACROSS THE WESTERN FRONT; A CRUCIAL MEETING IN VERDUN; A LINE ON THE MAP (PAGES 86-105)

- How did General Eisenhower's reaction to the initial attacks in the Ardennes differ from General Bradley's? What measures did Eisenhower take to defend the area?
- What contributed to the end of the German airborne operations?
- How did the Germans attempt to infiltrate the American lines?
- How did the Americans thwart German sabotage efforts?

- When General Eisenhower met with his generals in Verdun, he said, "The present situation is to be regarded as one of opportunity for us and not of disaster" (p. 97). What message was he trying to convey?
- What was his tactical approach to stop the Germans?
- What did Eisenhower's decision to turn over leadership of two American armies to British Field Marshal Montgomery reveal about him as a leader?

BASTOGNE: THE LEFT FLANK; "NUTS"; ST.-VITH: THE RIGHT FLANK; THE ALLIES' SECRET WEAPON; TRACKING THE MONSTER (PAGES 109–139)

- What obstacles did the 101st Airborne face in its defense of Bastogne?
- How was the German request that the Americans surrender at Bastogne an empty threat?
- What gave General McAuliffe the confidence to turn this offer down?
- Despite the withdrawal and heavy losses of Allied troops at St.-Vith, how had the Allies impacted Germany's plans?
- How was the invention of the fuse called the "pozit" a secret weapon for the Allies?
- How did the Allies stop Lieutenant Colonel Peiper's drive toward the Meuse?

STATUS: GERMANY; STATUS: ALLIED FORCES; BASTOGNE: SATURDAY, DECEMBER 23, 1944; "XMAS PRESENT COMING"; PATTON: LUXEMBOURG CITY (PAGES 140–152)

- What was the status of the German and Allied forces in the days before Christmas 1944?
- How had things changed for the Americans trapped in Bastogne?
- What was the significance to the Americans of the Allied victory in Bastogne?
- What effect did this victory have on the Germans?

"GLORY HAS ITS PRICE"; INSURRECTION IN THE NORTH; INSURRECTION IN THE SOUTH; THE LAST GERMAN GROUND OFFENSIVE; THE INTERNAL FIGHT FOR STRASBOURG (PAGES 153-177)

- How were the Allied commanders divided in their approach to defeating the Germans?
- What caused friction between General Eisenhower and Field Marshal Montgomery?
- What problems did Eisenhower face on the southern flank?
- What was the German plan after the failure of Autumn Mist? Was it successful? Explain.
- How did the defense of Strasbourg create discord between American and French leaders?

WINSTON CHURCHILL ARRIVES; NEW WORRIES; YARD BY YARD; "I KNOW THE WAR IS LOST" (PAGES 178-195)

- How did political issues affect Eisenhower's decisions regarding the defense of Strasbourg?
- What military concerns and losses plagued General Eisenhower at this time?
- How did the Allies regain control of the western half of the bulge "yard by yard"?
- How did the Allied victory in the Battle of the Bulge contribute to Germany's defeat in the war?
- What were the Allied and German casualties and losses in this conflict?

EPILOGUE (PAGES 196-200)

- How did Hitler's Autumn Mist plan have the opposite outcome from what he had hoped?
- How does the author's claim that "war is never linear, but rather a chaotic, haphazard enterprise of reversal and advance, blunder and enthusiasm, despair and elation" (p. 200) describe the Battle of the Bulge?

THEY CAME BY SEA AND BY SKY to reclaim liberty from the occupying Germans. As the Allied forces stormed the beaches of Normandy, they turned the tide of World War II.

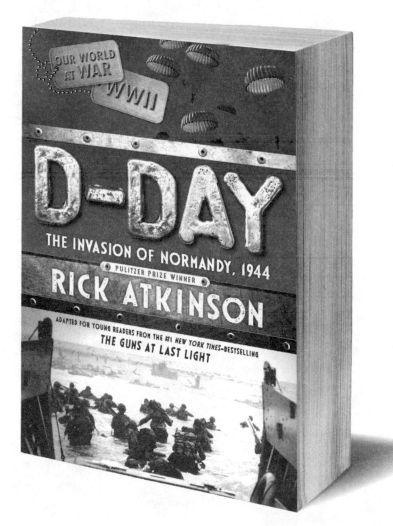

Keep reading for an excerpt.

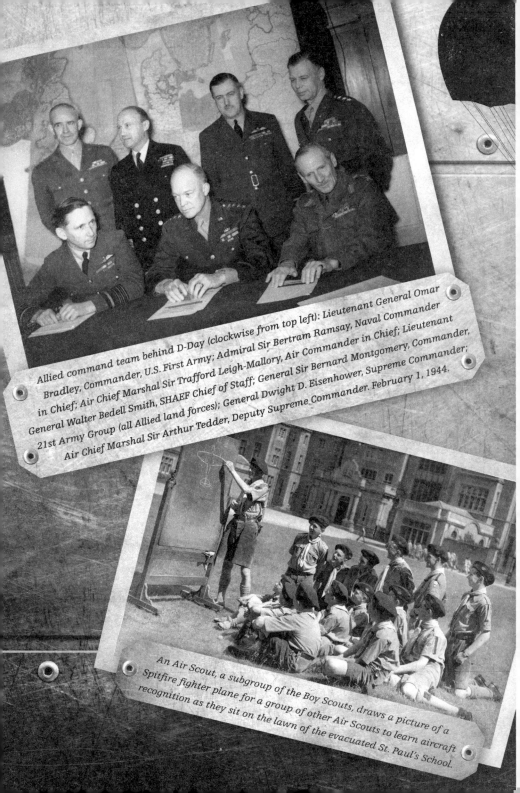

Allied command team behind D-Day (clockwise from top left): Lieutenant General Omar Bradley, Commander, U.S. First Army; Admiral Sir Bertram Ramsay, Naval Commander in Chief; Air Chief Marshal Sir Trafford Leigh-Mallory, Air Commander in Chief; Lieutenant General Walter Bedell Smith, SHAEF Chief of Staff; General Sir Bernard Montgomery, Commander, 21st Army Group (all Allied land forces); General Dwight D. Eisenhower, Supreme Commander; Air Chief Marshal Sir Arthur Tedder, Deputy Supreme Commander. February 1, 1944.

An Air Scout, a subgroup of the Boy Scouts, draws a picture of a Spitfire fighter plane for a group of other Air Scouts to learn aircraft recognition as they sit on the lawn of the evacuated St. Paul's School.

THE
GATHERING
MAY 5, 1944

IN THIS ROOM, the greatest Anglo-American military leaders of World War II gathered to rehearse the deathblow intended to destroy Adolf Hitler's Third Reich. It was the 1,720th day of the war. Admirals, generals, field marshals, logisticians, and staff by the score climbed from their limousines and marched into a Gothic building of St. Paul's School. American military policemen—known as Snowdrops for their white helmets, white pistol belts, white leggings, and white gloves—looked closely at the 146 engraved invitations and security passes distributed a month earlier. Then six uniformed ushers escorted the guests, later described as "big men with the air of fame about them," into the Model Room, a cold auditorium with black columns and hard, narrow benches reputedly designed to keep young schoolboys awake. The students of St. Paul's School had long been evacuated to rural England—German bombs had shattered seven hundred windows across the school's campus.

Top-secret charts and maps now lined the Model Room. Since January, the school had served as headquarters for the British 21st Army Group, and here the detailed planning for Operation OVERLORD, the Allied invasion of France, had gelled. As the senior officers found their benches in rows B through J, some spread blankets across their laps or cinched their overcoats against the chill. Row A, fourteen armchairs arranged elbow to elbow, was reserved for the highest of the mighty, and now these men began to take their seats. The prime minister of England, Winston Churchill, dressed in a black coat and

Air Chief Marshal Sir Sholto Douglass (left) standing with his senior air staff officer in the operations room on the morning of the invasion.

holding his usual Havana cigar, entered with U.S. General Dwight D. Eisenhower, whose title, Supreme Commander of the Allied Expeditionary Force, signaled his leadership over all of the Allied forces in Europe. Neither cheers nor applause greeted them, but the assembly stood as one when King George VI strolled down the aisle to sit on Eisenhower's right. Churchill bowed

His Imperial Majesty King George VI

to his monarch, then resumed puffing his cigar.

As they waited to begin at the stroke of ten A.M., these big men with their air of importance had reason to rejoice in their joint victories and to hope for greater victories still to come in this war.

Sir Winston Churchill, prime minister of the United Kingdom, inspecting a crater left by a German bomb in London, September 10, 1940.

Since September 1939, war had raged across Europe, eventually spreading to North Africa and as far east as Moscow, capital of the Soviet Union. Germany, a country humiliated after World War I, had seen the rise of Adolf Hitler, a dictator who had dreams of conquering the continent. Beginning with Poland, his armies had crushed one nation after another, destroying cities and killing or enslaving millions of people. His collaborators in the Axis alliance, particularly Japan and Italy, pushed their own campaigns of aggression in Asia and Africa.

Hitler's invasion of the Soviet Union in June 1941, and Japan's attack in December of that year on the U.S. naval base at Pearl Harbor in Hawaii, led to a grand alliance determined to stop the Axis. The United States, Great Britain, and the Soviet Union were the major Allied powers, but they were supported

Adolf Hitler, führer of the Nazi Party (right), and Benito Mussolini, prime minister of Italy, in Munich, Germany, June 1940.

The U.S.S. Shaw explodes during the Japanese attack on Pearl Harbor, December 7, 1941.

by dozens of other countries. At an enormous cost in blood, Soviet armies pushed the German invaders back through eastern Europe, mile by mile. German casualties there exceeded three million, and in 1944 nearly two-thirds of Hitler's combat power remained tied up in the east.

The United States and Britain, meanwhile, had defeated German and Italian forces in North Africa. They then moved north across the Mediterranean Sea to conquer much of Italy, which surrendered and abandoned the Axis. The Third Reich, as Hitler called his empire, was ever more vulnerable to air attack. Allied planes flying from Britain, Italy, and Africa dropped thousands of tons of bombs on Germany and on German forces along various battle fronts. City by city, factory

*A U.S. propaganda poster encourages increased
production prior to D-Day, 1943–1944.*

by factory, Germany was a country increasingly in flames.
Although they paid a staggering cost in airplanes and flight
crews, the U.S. Army Air Forces, Britain's Royal Air Force, and
the Canadian Air Force had won mastery of the European skies,
even as Allied navies controlled the seas.

By the late spring of 1944, the Allies were ready to attempt
something that had long seemed impossible: to invade what
the Germans called "Fortress Europe" and begin the final campaign that would free citizens who had been enslaved since
Germany invaded Poland on September 1, 1939. The hour of
liberation had nearly arrived.

BIBLIOGRAPHY

THIS BOOK IS A VERSION of an adult book called *The Guns at Last Light*, part of my Liberation Trilogy. Below are several titles from the complete bibliography for the trilogy. A complete list, with comments, is available at liberationtrilogy.com/books/wwii-resources.

For a big-picture understanding of the global war, I recommend *A World at Arms* by Gerhard L. Weinberg, *Inferno: The World at War, 1939–1945* by Max Hastings, *The Second World War* by Antony Beevor, *A War to Be Won* by Williamson Murray and Allan R. Millett, *The Struggle for Europe* by Chester Wilmot, and *Why the Allies Won* by Richard Overy.

Perhaps the most vivid and tactile account of the war can be found at the National World War II Museum in New Orleans. Over the past decade, the museum has vastly expanded its artifacts, pavilions, and archival holdings; it now offers a thorough, compelling experience about the war's origins, campaigns, personalities, and consequences. For more information, visit the Web site at nationalww2museum.org.

IMAGE CREDITS

INDEX

(Page references in *italic* refer to illustrations.)